# The
# RUSSIAN
# WAY

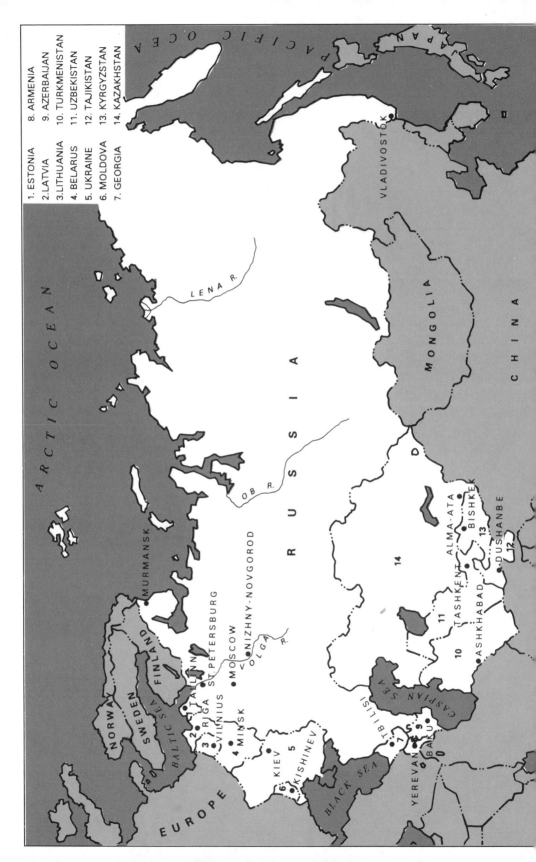

# The RUSSIAN WAY

*Aspects of Behavior,*

*Attitudes, and Customs*

*of the Russians*

## ZITA DABARS
### with LILIA VOKHMINA

*Printed on recyclable paper*

**PASSPORT BOOKS**
a division of *NTC Publishing Group*
Lincolnwood, Illinois USA

Cover photos courtesy of Zita D. Dabars

**1996 Printing**

Published by Passport Books, a division of NTC Publishing Group.
© 1995 by NTC Publishing Group, 4255 West Touhy Avenue,
Lincolnwood (Chicago), Illinois 60646-1975 U.S.A.
Manufactured in the United States of America.

5 6 7 8 9 0 VP 9 8 7 6 5 4 3 2

# CONTENTS

CONTENTS

# INTRODUCTION

Every country has its Culture with a "capital C." For Russia, Tchaikovsky, Chekhov and Solzhenitsyn, and icons are representative of its music, literature, and art. Although it is this "Culture" that first comes to mind, every country also has its "small c" culture, which includes the customs and conventions of its people. A knowledge of the habits and practices of the Russian people provides answers to such questions as:

- What items do Russians consider appropriate presents? Why would a young man wooing a Russian girl make the wrong impression by presenting a birthday gift of six yellow roses?

- Why should visitors in a Russian apartment partake sparingly of the cold cuts and salads on the table when they sit down for a meal?

- What does it mean when a black border surrounds one of the names on a list of coauthors in a book?

While in a conversation with an Intourist guide in the former Soviet Union, I took out my calendar to jot down a schedule change. To emphasize what dates the group would be in the country, I had outlined March 16–30 in pen. Upon seeing the calendar, the Intourist guide asked in a hurt voice, "Why would you outline the dates you are in the Soviet Union in black?" I learned then that it is a Russian custom to put a black border around the printed names of people who have died. Of course on future trips, I no longer outlined the dates in black.

Whether the nature of the relationship with a foreign culture is business, professional, or that of a casual tourist, the more sensitivity we have toward the culture's habits, customs, and mores, the greater our satisfaction and pleasure will be.

Scholars who have examined how people react to another culture have found numerous levels of perception. In *Teaching Language in Context* (Boston: Heinle & Heinle, 1993, page 371) Alice Omaggio Hadley presents the levels of cross-cultural awareness developed by Robert Hanley and described by Vicki Galloway at the Northeast Conference on the Teaching of Foreign Languages 1985 Winter Workshop.

Level I: Information about the culture may consist of superficial or visible traits, such as isolated facts or stereotypes. The individual very likely sees the culture as odd, bizarre, and exotic. Ideas are often expressed in terms of what the culture lacks. Culture bearers may be considered rude, ignorant, or unrefined at this stage of understanding.

Level II: Learners at this stage focus on expanded knowledge about the culture in terms of both significant and subtle traits that contrast with those of their own culture. The learners might find the culture bearers' behavior irrational, frustrating, irritating, or nonsensical.

Level III: At this stage, the individual begins to accept the culture at an intellectual level, and thus the culture becomes believable because it can be explained. The individual can see things in terms of the target culture's frame of reference.

Level IV: This level, the level of empathy, is achieved through living in and through the culture. The individual begins to see the culture from the viewpoint of the insider, and thus is able to know how the culture bearer feels.

The aim of *The Russian Way* is to help students, teachers, business travelers, diplomats, and tourists—active or armchair—

reach the Level III stage of cultural awareness. Winston Churchill described Russia as "a riddle wrapped in a mystery inside an enigma;" and the nineteenth century Russian poet Fyodor Tyutchev wrote: "Russia cannot be understood with the mind . . . One must simply believe in Russia." But there are ways of understanding Russia and the Russians by utilizing knowledge and information about the country. Russians do things in a particular way—a way that may be similar or different from the ways of Americans. Similar or different—not right or wrong. An awareness of these behaviors removes some of the mystery. Just as our appreciation of a painting in a museum is enhanced by knowing something about art, the more knowledge we bring to a culture, the deeper our understanding is of that culture and its people.

A note on the translation and transliteration of Russian words in *The Russian Way*: All Russian words and phrases appear in Cyrillic, accompanied by a transliteration of the Cyrillic word or phrase and the English translation. In words with two or more syllables, italics indicate which syllable is stressed. The transliteration system used is the one approved by the U.S. Board on Geographic Names, with a few minor alterations to aid the reader in pronunciation.

# ACKNOWLEDGMENTS

*The Russian Way* manuscript has benefited from suggestions by colleagues and friends in both the United States and the former Soviet Union. In the United States, it was read by Ilya Evstifeev, Melissa Feliciano (Friends School, Baltimore), Steve Frank, Mikhail Gipsov, Olga Hutchins, Aleksandr Jacobson, Taj Johnson, Thora Johnson, Irina Kotok, and George Morris (St. Louis University High School). In Russia, Irina Vorontsova (School #15, Moscow), Emil Vorontsov and Pyotr Nikolaev (Moscow State University) critiqued portions of the manuscript.

## ACKNOWLEDGMENTS

Throughout the years, many organizations have enabled me to study, do research, and travel in the former Soviet Union, and grateful thanks is extended to them. The International Research and Educational Exchange (IREX) arranged for teachers to study during summers at Moscow State University. Promoting Enduring Peace sponsored study tours for high school students before it became common practice to do so. The Geraldine R. Dodge Foundation funded the developmental costs of the writing of the *Russian Face to Face* series, enabling the bilateral team of coauthors to work and live in each other's homes. The Partnership Exchange Program of the American Council of Teachers of Russian (ACTR), funded by the United States Information Agency, allowed my students and me to study and teach at School #15 in Moscow and to live with Russian families. My work at Friends School in Baltimore and at its Center of Russian Language and Culture (CORLAC) has given me the opportunity to present the complexities of Russia to the Friends School community and beyond.

This book is dedicated to the people of Russia: the passerby who took the time to go out of his or her way when I asked for directions, the Intourist guides who were able to convey their love of their country despite the restrictions, and the colleagues and friends who showed me the beauty of their country, the wealth of their culture, and the richness of their history, and who shared with me their professional concerns and invited me into their kitchens.

# 1. ABBREVIATIONS AND ACRONYMS

There are times in a conversation when a non-native speaker understands a native Russian-speaker quite well until something unexpectedly perplexing is said. Often the incomprehensible word turns out to be an abbreviation or an acronym.

An abbreviation is a shortened form of a word or phrase which is generally, but not always, followed by a period. Some typical English abbreviations are:

| | |
|---|---|
| p. | pint, page |
| a.m. | ante meridiem |
| sq. yd. | square yard |
| USA | United States of America |

In *The Russian's World,* Genevra Gerhart devotes an entire section (pp. 211–225) to the topic of abbreviations and acronyms in Russian. Her classifications are used in the following section.

## Russian abbreviations, *sokrashcheniya (сокращéния)*

Russian abbreviations are formed by the first letter of a word, by the first few letters of a word, or by the first letter of each word in a phrase. The abbreviations may be written with or without a period, in small or capital letters.

The following abbreviations are sometimes called *literary* (or conventional) abbreviations "us*lov*niye sokra*shche*niya" (**услóвные сокращéния**), because they are encountered only in written form.

**POINT 1**

(For the pronunciation of Russian letters, see Point 51, "*The Russian Language.*")

| | | |
|---|---|---|
| century | **в./v.** | **век**/vek |
| Women's room | **Ж/Zh** | **Же́нская (убо́рная)**/ *Zhenskaya (ubornaya)* |
| and so forth | **и т.д./i t.d.** | **и так да́лее** / *i tak dalee* |
| mainly, for the most part | **гл. обр./gl. obr.** | **гла́вным о́бразом** / *glavnym obrazom* |
| deputy, substitute | **зам./zam.** | **замести́тель** / *zamestitel* |

*Letter* abbreviations, "*Buk*venniye sokra*shche*niya" (**Бу́квенные сокраще́ния**), use the first letter of each word in the names of countries, organizations, factories, and educational institutions. These abbreviations appear in written form and also are used in speech. It is important to know how to pronounce them and whether they should be declined, i.e., inflected, depending on the role they play in a sentence.

| | | | |
|---|---|---|---|
| Moscow State University | **МГУ/MGU** [pronounced "em-ge-u"] | **Моско́вский госуда́рственный университе́т** | Mo*sk*ovskiy gosu*da*rstvenniy universi*ty*et |
| United States of America | **США/SSHA** [pronounced "se-sha-a"] | **Соединённые Шта́ты Аме́рики** | Soyedin*nyo*nniye *Shta*ty A*me*riki |
| United Nations | **ООН/OON** [pronounced "o-o-en"] | **Организа́ция Объединённых На́ций** | Organi*zats*iya Obyedi*nyo*nnykh *Na*tsiy |
| Moscow automobile plant named in honor of Likhachov | **ЗИЛ/ZIL** [pronounced "zil"] | **Заво́д и́мени Лихачёва** | Za*v*od *i*meni Likha*cho*va |
| Acquired immune deficiency syndrome (AIDS) | **СПИД/SPID** [pronounced "speed"] | **Синдро́м приобретённого иммунодефици́та** | Sind*rom* priobre*tyon*novo immunodefi*ts*ita |

## Russian acronyms

Acronyms, "slozhnosokra*shchyo*nniye slo*va*"/**сложносокращённые слова́**, are words formed from:

1.  the initial syllables of two or more words, e.g.,

    | (school) department head or vice-principal | **за́вуч**/*za*vuch | from **заве́дующий**/<br>za*ve*duyushchiy<br>manager, chief |
    | --- | --- | --- |
    | | | **уче́бной ча́стью**/<br>u*che*bnoy *cha*styu<br>director of<br>students, depart-<br>ment head, or vice-<br>principal |

2.  the initial syllable of one word plus another whole word, e.g.,

    | nurse | **медсестра́**/<br>medse*stra* | from **медици́нский**/<br>medi*tsin*skiy,<br>medical, and<br>**сестра́**/sestr*a*,<br>sister |
    | --- | --- | --- |
    | salary, pay | **зарпла́та**/<br>zar*pla*ta | from **за́работная<br>пла́та**/*za*rabotnaya<br>*pla*ta, salary |
    | office supplies | **канцтова́ры**/<br>kantsto*va*ry | from **канцеля́рские<br>това́ры** /<br>kantse*lya*rskiye<br>to*va*ry, office<br>supplies |

3.  the initial syllable of one word plus a *letter* abbreviation, e.g.,

    | city department of public education | **ГорОНО**/<br>GorONO | from **городско́й<br>отде́л наро́дного<br>образова́ния**/<br>gorod*skoy* ot*del*<br>na*rod*novo<br>obrazo*va*niya, city<br>department of<br>public education |
    | --- | --- | --- |

## 2. ADVERTISING

Until 1985 advertising was almost nonexistent in Russia (and other former Soviet countries), since the economic system was not based on competition. Manufactured goods were produced and distributed on the basis of governmental and party plans or command economics. Even though "Save Money in Banks" and "Fly Aeroflot" could be seen on the sides of buildings, there was no competition among banks or airline companies because there was only one state bank and one airline company in Russia. To encourage the purchase of insurance, the state insurance company, "Goss*trakh*"/ **Госстрáх**, advertised on television. Except for the Pepsi soft drink company, ads for foreign products were nonexistent.

After 1985, individuals were allowed to organize cooperatives in manufacturing and service industries. Small businesses sprang up, markets opened, and local as well as international competition began. As a result, ads started to appear on billboards, in newspapers, and in magazines. For the first time television and radio programs were interrupted by commercials. Japanese and South Korean companies led the way with advertising for electronic and automotive products. Today many such ads are in English, directed toward people with American dollars. The Russian ads of the 1990s promote mainly banks, imports, the sale and service of computers and cars, and the sale or renting of houses and apartments. Currently, it appears that all of Russia is besieged by the Mars Company's ads pitching Snickers candy bars.

In 1993 a law was passed stating that although foreign companies operating in Russia, such as McDonald's, Estée Lauder, Gucci, and Levi Strauss, could have their logos displayed in their native language, they were also required to have their logos prominently displayed in Cyrillic.

# 3.  APPROACHING STRANGERS IN PUBLIC TO ASK FOR INFORMATION

To attract someone's attention to ask for directions, for the cost of an item, or about transportation, address the person by saying "Izvi*ni*te, po*zha*luista," Excuse me, please (**Извини́те, пожа́луйста**), "Ska*zhi*te, po*zha*luista," Tell me, please (**Скажи́те, пожа́луйста**), or simply "Po*zha*luista," Please (**Пожа́луйста**). Indeed, "po*zha*luista," please (**пожа́луйста**), is a most useful Russian word to ask for help, thank someone, or invite someone to the table.

"Izvi*ni*te," Excuse me (**извини́те**), can be used to attract someone's attention as well as to apologize for some minor transgression. If you are mistaken for a Russian and are approached with a question in Russian just say, "Izvi*ni*te, ya ne govo*ryu* po-*rus*ski," Excuse me, I don't speak Russian (**Извини́те, я не говорю́ по-ру́сски**).

# 4.  AT THE TABLE

If you are invited for dinner at someone's home, expect to be seated at the table. Cocktail parties and buffet dinners where guests eat standing are not common in Russia, although they are becoming more frequent as more Western and other companies conduct business in Russia.

Russian generosity is justly renowned. Even in a dire economy, be prepared for an impressive spread when invited to a Russian home. And no one will mention that half a month's salary has been spent on the meal! In response to the invitation "Pro*shu* k sto*ly*," Please [come] to the table (**Прошу́ к столу́**), everyone will sit down. As they begin to eat, Russians will wish their dining companions "Pri*yat*novo appe*ti*ta," Bon appétit! (**Прия́тного аппети́та**).

The Russian table setting places the fork on the left side of the plate, the knife and the soup spoon on the right, and the teaspoon above the plate. Dinner-size plates are used for the main course of a dinner, but smaller salad or dessert plates are used for breakfast and lunch. Russians hold the fork in the left hand, the knife in the right. Desserts such as cakes are eaten with a spoon, not a fork. It is not considered impolite to reach for food across the table (with one's hand or fork) to pick up bread or to spear a pickle. When not being used, the utensil end of knives and forks are placed on the plates, with the tines of the forks down. To indicate you have finished a meal, place the fork and knife parallel in the middle of the plate. It is considered polite to leave a bit of food on the plate.

# 5.   ATTRACTING SOMEONE'S ATTENTION

Since the 1917 Revolution, it has been considered inappropriate to use the Russian terms for Mr., "gospo*din*" (**господи́н**), Mrs. or Miss, "gospo*zha*" (**госпожа́**) and Ladies and Gentlemen, "gospo*da*" (**господа́**). The new terms "grazhda*nin*," "grazh*dan*ka," "grazh*dan*ye," and "to*va*rishch," citizen, citiziness, citizens, and comrade (**граждани́н, гражда́нка, гра́ждане,** and **това́рищ**), were used instead although they were official and sometimes sounded a bit artificial. In the 1990s, "gospo*din*," Mr. (**господи́н**), "gospo*zha*," Mrs. or Miss (**госпожа́**), and "gospo*da*," Ladies and Gentlemen (**господа́**), appeared to be regaining favor—especially in financial circles—even among Russians. At times, the English words Mr., Mrs., and Miss are used in addressing foreigners.

To attact the attention of a saleslady or a waitress, it is appropriate to call out "*dye*vushka," girl (**де́вушка**) to a female aged 15 to 50. In recent years, the words "*pa*ren," fellow (**па́рень**), "molo*doy*chelo*vek*," young man (**молодо́й челове́к**), "muzh*chi*na," man (**мужчи́на**), and "*zhen*shchina," woman (**же́нщина**), are widely used, although cated Russians consider this practice low-class. An unknown older man may be referred to as "*dya*dya," uncle (дя́дя).

# 6. *BABUSHKA*, GRANDMOTHER (*БАБУШКА*)

Grandmothers, more frequently than in the West, live with one of their children, not only due to housing shortages but because of the closeness of the Russian extended family. Especially if she is retired, a babushka is the main helper in the family, preparing meals, babysitting, shopping, and even assisting with the grandchildren's homework. Grandmothers also act as commentators on social behavior, reprimanding those they consider to be out of line. They can be found in all kinds of weather sitting on benches in front of their homes in the countryside or at the entrances to apartment buildings in the city.

# 7. BALLET AND THE RUSSIAN THEATER

Although ballet originated in the court of Louis XIV of France, its glory days came when it grew in Russian soil. Empress Elizabeth, Peter the Great's daughter, created a court school in St. Petersburg in the eighteenth century, and by Pushkin's day in the nineteenth century ballet had reached a position of significant artistic importance. In the twentieth century, it is impossible to conceive of a diplomatic mission to Moscow without the requisite evening at the Bolshoi Theater, preferably to see "Lebe*di*noe *oz*ero," *Swan Lake*

(**Лебеди́ное о́зеро**). Indeed, tickets to Moscow's Bolshoi Theater or St. Petersburg's Mariinsky Theater (Leningrad's Kirov Theater) were greatly valued as bribes during much of the Soviet period.

The following appears on a ticket to a Russian performance: the name of the theater, the date of the production, the name of the production (stamped, i.e., not printed, on the ticket), and the location of the seat in the theater. A ticket with "part*yer*," orchestra seats (**партéр**), "*lye*vaya storo*na*" left side (**лéвая сторонá**), "ryad 2," row 2 (**ряд 2**), "*mye*sto 16," place 16 (**мéсто** 16), indicates that the ticket is for the left side of the orchestra, row 2, seat 16. "*Pra*vaya storo*na*" would send the theatergoer to the right side (**прáвая сторонá**). Other terms used in traditional opera/ballet theaters to designate seats are, in ascending order: seats on the same level as the orchestra seats, but behind and around them (lower boxes— "benu*ar*" (**бенуáр**); the tier immediately above this level (dress circle)—"bele*tazh*" (**бельэтáж**); the tiers above these two levels— "*ya*rus" (**я́рус**); the last balcony (the gallery)—"gale*re*ya" (**галерéя**). "*Lo*zha" (**лóжа**) indicates that the seat is in a box. Newer theaters designate the less expensive orchestra seats—"amfite*atr*" (**амфитеáтр**), and the balcony—"bal*kon*" (**балкóн**). (It is wise to be in your seat at the start of a performance; once the performance begins, latecomers are not seated until there is a significant break in the action on stage, or possibly only at the end of the first act. Latecomers are sometimes seated in unoccupied balcony seats until the end of the first act. It is also common for Russians to move into better, unoccupied seats once a performance starts.)

Whereas in the United States there is usually a free theater program full of information about the performance and the cast, plus advertising geared for a theatergoing audience, in Russia there is a minimal charge for a two- or four-page program giving the most essential information—scenes, acts, and cast member names.

In addition to ordinary applause, Russians often express pleasure by rhythmic clapping. Shouts of *Bravo!* and *Brava!* greet popular performers. As elsewhere, favorite performers are presented with flowers. At theaters such as the Bolshoi or the Mariinsky (Kirov), the flowers are presented by ushers on stage, or they are thrown onto the stage by fans. When an orchestra pit does not prevent the fans from approaching the stage, fans hand flowers directly to the performers. While the fans are applauding, frequently the performers themselves will also applaud, signifying appreciation for the audience. As in most of Europe, fans express displeasure by whistling. During intermissions, many theaters have a public room in which theatergoers, arm in arm, promenade, walking round and round the room. Others head for the theater's buffets. Because most evening performances begin at seven o'clock, theatergoers do not have time to eat dinner at home. Open-faced caviar, salami, or smoked fish sandwiches, pastries, and chocolate—washed down with juice or champagne (served in real glasses as opposed to plastic ones)—help assuage hunger and make the occasion a festive one. When delicacies are scarce elsewhere, they can generally be found at theaters.

When Russians enter a row with people already seated in it, they face those seated rather than the stage, and proceed across the row. To do otherwise, i.e., to face the stage, is considered impolite because one's back side then faces those seated.

Coats, hats, or rubber overshoes may not be worn in the seating area of Russian theaters (or in places such as museums and restaurants). They must be left at the "garde*rob*," cloakroom (гардероб). There is no charge for this service, and kind cloakroom attendants have been known to repair a loose "*ve*shalka," loop near the coat collar (вѐшалка) that is used to hang up the coat. After the removal of hats and coats, public primping at the mirrors provided in the coatroom is an accepted practice. When the performance is over, people line up to retrieve their coats. To avoid standing in line, patrons frequently rent binoculars at a modest cost, even if they have excellent seats, because returning the binoculars assures a quick move to the front of the coat line. In movie theaters and at sporting events Russians keep their coats on.

# 8. *BANYA*, THE RUSSIAN SAUNA *(БА́НЯ)*

The tradition of the Russian sauna is very old; it is known to have existed in the Middle Ages. Until the 1917 Bolshevik Revolution almost every Russian village house had its own *banya*, separate from the main house. Eighty percent of the population lived in villages. The *banya* was built close to a water supply such as a river, a lake, or a town well. The temperature inside a *banya* is heated by the use of wood-burning stoves. Water is boiled in kettles and poured on heated stones. The resulting moist hot air is different from the dry heat of Finnish saunas. In a *banya* people sit or lie naked on benches and beat themselves with a birch or oak switch called a *"vyenik"* (ве́ник). To protect their hair, men wear woolen hats, and women, if they can, braid their hair. Men and women take turns using the *banya*. Afterwards people jump into the cold water of a lake or river or roll around in the snow.

Communal baths are located in cities and towns. The demand for them originally came from factories. After bathing, instead of jumping into a lake or river, as in the country, people douse themselves with cold water from a bucket, or in the case of modern *banyas*, from a shower. These types of *banyas* are divided into four parts. People undress in the "pred*ba*nnik," dressing room (предба́нник). There is a "*mo*echnaya," washing room (мо́ечная), sometimes called a "dushe*va*ya" (душева́я). Afterwards, people head for the "pa*ri*lka," the steam room (пари́лка). They sit on stone benches (as expected, the higher they choose to sit, the hotter the air) and beat themselves, as described above. The humid air is so hot that one can stay there only for limited periods of time. In the steam room people sit, drink tea, beer, or vodka, play chess, or chat.

At present, even though most apartments have bathrooms, *banyas* continue to enjoy great popularity. Their attraction lies in the fact that not only are they a source for cleanliness, but perhaps even more importantly, they provide a place for people to gather for social pleasure.

# 9. BRIBERY AND *BLAT*, "PULL" (*БЛАТ*)

Bribery has always been a frequent practice in Russia (as in many other countries). Even during the time of the tsars, Russian officials excelled at bribery. In the nineteenth-century satirical play, *The Inspector General*, Revizor, one of Nikolai Gogol's characters, accuses another of "taking more than is your due;" he does not criticize him for bribery as such. "Ne pod*ma*zhesh, ne po*ye*desh," If you don't oil [i.e., give a bribe], you cannot start your journey (**Не подмáжешь, не поéдешь**), is an old Russian proverb. Bribes are offered to get a child into a university, to obtain a good job, to help a business, and to avoid army service.

During the time of Stalin, bribery was less widespread than at other times in Russia's history. Laws are strictly enforced under despots. If there is a choice between "life" or "a bribe," most people choose life and avoid bribes. Since the 1960s bribery has become more prevalent, because laws are less strictly enforced and there is a scarcity of goods and services.

*Blat*, which can be best translated as "pull," "influence," or "connections," has always been important in Russia. As in many other countries, it is not important what you know, but who you know. Even in everyday life it is almost impossible to accomplish something if you do not have contacts—"svo*ya* ru*ka*" or "*la*pa" (**своя́ рукá** or **лáпа**)—in the right places. Want an airline (or train) ticket, a reservation in a hotel or in a restaurant, a ticket to a special theater performance, a permit for the opening of a business venture or for construction? It is absolutely necessary to know where to turn, and what "token"—not a bribe, but a souvenir, or a gift of appreciation—to present to whom. Depending on what "favor" is needed, these "gifts" can vary—a package of cigarettes (Marlboro is the most popular), toys, a bottle of Scotch or bourbon, cosmetics, a computer, or a ticket to the USA. It is possible that people you meet at first in formal, "bribetaking" situations may with time become your personal "friends" and that you will exchange favors on a regular basis.

# 10. THE CALENDAR

Like the European calendar, the Russian calendar week starts with Monday and ends with Sunday. The names of the days reflect this fact: "*vto*nik," Tuesday (**вто́рник**), comes from "vto*roy*," **второ́й** second [day of the week]. Russian calendars generally are aligned up and down, not left to right. Pocketbook-size calendars with a tear-off page per day are popular in Russia. The calendars are labeled "for women," "for schoolchildren," etc. For each day there is reading material of interest to those for whom the calendars are intended.

Since 1918 Russia has followed the Gregorian calendar; previously the Julian calendar was used. Consequently, the October Revolution, which took place on October 25, 1917, by the Julian calendar, after 1918 was celebrated on November 7th. The Russian Orthodox Church continues to follow the Julian calendar; hence Christmas is celebrated not on December 25th, but on January 7th by Russian Christians.

# 11. CELEBRATIONS AND HOLIDAYS

Russians have always loved to celebrate. During tsarist times, the holidays were associated with the Russian Orthodox religion, the reign of the Romanovs, and the special personal days of the reigning tsar's family. Life in the village revolved around the church calendar. Peasants plowed on St. George's Day in May and picked apples on Transfiguration Day in August. After the October 1917 Revolution, religious holidays were frequently replaced by official secular holidays.

Of the church holidays, Easter *(Pa*skha/**Па́сха**) in contrast to the West's Christmas, is the most significant. Before the 1917

Bolshevik Revolution, Easter followed Lent, a seven-week period of strict fasting. Today, fasting is not widespread. However, even the nonreligious observe Easter. In the evening people begin to gather in churches. The traditional Easter foods, "ku*lich*," an Easter cake similar to sweet bread (**кули́ч**), "*pas*kha," an Easter dessert similar to cheesecake (**па́сха**), and colored Easter eggs, known as "*kra*shenniye *yai*tsa" (**кра́шенные я́йца,** or in Ukrainian "*pis*anki," **пи́санки**), are presented to the priests to be blessed. The official celebration of Easter begins at midnight on Saturday and continues into Sunday. An especially festive church service is conducted, and there is a church procession. The entire congregation, which is especially well represented at this holiday, follows the priests with icons, banners, and incense. After midnight and throughout the next day, people kiss each other three times. They say "Khris*tos* vos*kres*e," Christ has risen (**Христо́с воскре́се**), and the answer given is "Vo*is*tinu vos*kres*e," Truly He has risen (**Вои́стину воскре́се**). After the church service, the fast is broken with a sumptuous feast.

Other secular and religious holidays are:

| January 1 | New Year's Day | *No*vy god | **Но́вый год** |
|---|---|---|---|
| January 7 | Christmas [Russian Orthodox] | Rozhdest*vo* | **Рождество́** |
| March 8 | International Women's Day | Myezhduna*rod*niy *zhen*skiy dyen | **Междунаро́дный же́нский день** |
| May 9 | Victory Day | Dyen po*bye*dy | **День побе́ды** |
| June 12 | Russsian Independence Day | Dyen Neza*vi*simosti Ro*ssiy* | **День Незави́симости Росси́и** |
| October 7 | Constitution Day | Dyen Konsti*tut*siy | **День Конститу́ции** |

Following the 1917 Revolution, Christmas was no longer celebrated. It became an official holiday again in Russia only in 1993. Some offices and institutions celebrate both holidays, Russian Orthodox Christmas on January 7 and Western Christmas on December 25.

Like many European cultures, Russia has the equivalent of a

Santa Claus to help celebrate New Year's, and perhaps again soon, Christmas. "Dyed Mo*roz*," Grandfather Frost (**Дед Моро́з**) is generally taller than Santa and may wear either a blue or a red costume. At holiday parties, or "*yol*ki" (**ёлки**), he is frequently accompanied by "Snye*gu*rochka," Snowmaiden (**Снегу́рочка**), who helps him distribute presents. The name for the holiday party, "*yol*ka," comes from the Russian word for a fir tree. Peter the Great introduced the custom of decorating trees for the Christmas and New Year's holidays after his visit to Europe in the eighteenth century.

March 8, International Women's Day or simply Women's Day, is celebrated in Russia, but barely gets mentioned in U.S. newspapers. All women are honored on this day. On the day prior to the holiday, males give cards, gifts, and/or flowers to their fellow students, colleagues, and co-workers. On the actual holiday, families and friends gather, and gifts are proffered to the females present. While there is no equivalent holiday for men, women frequently congratulate and give cards and/or gifts to male acquaintances on February 23rd, known in the former Soviet Union as "Dyen So*vet*skoy A*r*mii i Vo*yen*no-Mor*sko*vo *Flo*ta," Soviet Army and Navy Day (**День Сове́тской А́рмии и Вое́нно-Морско́го Фло́та**).

Prior to 1993, two additional days were official holidays:

| May 1 | Workers International Solidarity Day | Dyen myezhduna*rod*njy soli*dar*nosti tru*dya*shchikhsya | **День междунаро́дной солида́рности трудя́щихся** |
|---|---|---|---|
| November 7 | Anniversary of the October 1917 Revolution | Godov*shchi*na Ok*tya*brskoy Revo*lyut*sii 1917 *go*da | **Годовщи́на Октя́брьской Револю́ции 1917 го́да** |

Even though May 1 is no longer an official holiday, it is still being celebrated by Russians as "*prazd*nik ve*sny*," spring holiday (**пра́здник весны́**).

As is the case in the United States where the observed day of a holiday is changed in order to give workers an extended weekend, a holiday in Russia may also be observed on another day. Moreover, if a holiday falls on a Tuesday, workers may be given the option of working on the preceding Saturday, so that they can be off the next Saturday, Sunday, Monday, and Tuesday. Russians who have country homes, or dachas (see Point 17), particularly appreciate these extended holidays. Anyone traveling to Russia on business should check the calendar for holidays to confirm any days that the business offices may be closed.

# 12. THE CIRCUS

The circus is a popular form of entertainment in Russia. The Russian circus emphasizes talent and skill, and the most popular acts feature acrobats, trapeze artists, clowns, and animals. Bears and horses appear most frequently, but elephants, tigers, lions, dogs, and even pigs and cats, are also featured.

Moscow has two circus buildings and two troupes. The older circus, recently renovated, features animal acts; the newer one, near Moscow State University, is famous for its trapeze artists, who fly high above the spectators. Russian circus performers always use safety nets.

When Russians want to indicate that things have gone out of whack, they say "Zhizn kak v *tsir*ke," Life is a circus (**Жизнь как в цирке**), just like we do in the United States.

# 13. CLOTHING

Clothing styles in Russia are in a state of flux. In general, Russians are more conservative in their dress than Americans. For example, in the 1970s, when pantsuits were popular in Europe and in America, young Russian women who wore them were severely criticized by the older generation. To this day, except for sports activities, shorts are not considered to be appropriate apparel, even in the hotter southern regions of Russia. Likewise, except for the younger generation, people dress in more somber colors than in the West. Having said this, however, it must be noted that in the mid-1990s a wide variety of clothing is seen on Russian streets and in the workplace because the demand for clothing is greater than the supply. People buy what is available and wear it, and the results may be bewildering. A secretary in an office might be wearing jeans—or a dress Westerners might consider more appropriate for evening wear. Russians often wear the same outfit for a number of days in a row.

In the 1990s, as Western clothing has become more available and affordable, newly rich Russians, especially in big cities, have been seen wearing fashionable quality clothing. Recognizable Western brands (Christian Dior, Calvin Klein, and Levi Strauss) are especially prized. Prior to the 1990s, quality clothing was scarce in Russia. Visitors wearing Western dress frequently received stares because of their fashionable clothes. Russians sometimes offered to buy the stylish Western clothing, referred to as "fir*ma*," **фирма́** in Russia. This was especially true of the famous brand-name items which have snob appeal and which in some circles enhance the owner's social status. Sometimes Russians refer to Western visitors as "fir*ma*."

From the 1970s to the early 1990s, of all Western apparel, jeans and clothing made from denim, were considered to be the height of fashion and an indication that the owner had "made it." Those Russians who chose to flaunt their status wore jeans to social functions for which a Westerner would not dress so casually.

Russians dressed in the latest fashion, "o*dety* v fir*mu*" **оде́ты в фирму́**, often become objects of envy and even attract thieves, much like in the West. Consequently, even if they can afford expensive clothing, some Russians frequently choose to wear it only in private. Fur hats are often snatched on the streets.

In addition to the popularity of quality Western clothing, there is a growing appreciation of Russia's own fashion industry. It is also true that many Russians throughout their lives sew their own clothes or rely on a dressmaker or a tailor ("port*noi*"/**портной**) to sew their clothing. "Do*ma mo*dy," Houses of fashion (**Дома́ мо́ды**) can be found in the larger cities of Russia. Slava Zaitsev, designer for Raisa Gorbachev, is probably the best known of the Russian designers. Responding to the new market economy of the 1990s, Russia's ready-to-wear industry is also experiencing an upsurge. Clothes with a "Made in Russia" label can now be found in American stores.

# 14. THE COLORS BLUE AND BROWN

Russians differentiate between shades of blue. Dark blue is "*si*niy"/ **си́ний**, and light blue is "golu*boy*"/**голубо́й**. The color brown has its own peculiarities. "Ko*rich*neviy"/**Кори́чневый** means "brown;" however, this word is never used to describe eye color. If someone's eyes are dark brown (almost black), they are referred to as "*cho*rniye"/ **чёрные**; light brown eyes are "*ka*riye"/**ка́рие**.

# 15. COMPLIMENTS

Americans are known throughout the world for their compliments. Russians, though less outgoing to strangers, also use expressions that convey praise. "Molo*dyets*!", Well done! [literally, Great fellow!] (**Молоде́ц**) is said to people of all ages and genders, not just to males. Russian and American reactions to compliments vary. When an American is paid a compliment, the typical reaction is to say "thanks"; a Russian, on the other hand, looks for an excuse to diminish the compliment. "Oh, thank you, but I've had this dress for ten years." In spite of such responses, compliments are much appreciated.

# 16. CRAFTS

Russia is renowned for the wealth of its arts and crafts. Most famous are its "*pa*lekh," lacquer boxes (**па́лех**) and brooches from the four villages of Palekh, Mstyora, Kholui, and Fedoskino; "khokhlo*ma*," painted woodenware (**хохлома́**) bowls, plates, spoons; Zhostovo trays; Pavlovsk wool shawls; Orenburg shawls made from mohair; Gzhel pottery, and Dymkov toys. Add to this list the ever popular Russian *matryoshkas* (nesting dolls), samovars, balalaikas, embroidered linens, carvings of bone, wood, and stone, wooden toys of people or animals that move, and you will understand why there is never a need for a Russian to give a present "Made in Hong Kong." The items mentioned above are so valued that a Russian will appreciate receiving them as gifts from a foreign visitor, in case you did not bring anything appropriate from home.

# 17. *DACHA*, COUNTRY HOUSE (ДА́ЧА)

Every Russian family living in the city strives to have its own dacha. Dachas provide a way to raise produce and escape from the city, with its bureaucracy, and other types of constraints. Although there was some variation by region, up until 1991 the maximum allowable size of the dacha area to be gardened ("sa*do*viy u*cha*stok"/**садóвый участок**) was 720 square yards; the maximum size for buildings, 30 square yards; and the maximum size for a patio, 12 square yards. In 1991 the limitations regarding the size and the quality of dachas were eliminated, and local authorities were given the right to set the maximum allowable area to be gardened. Russians took advantage of the new regulation, and today the results can be seen in the attractive houses which have sprung up throughout Russia. In 1993 more than half of Russia's population had some access to a dacha, and 20 million families have plots of land in the country. Russian dachas    are now more and more likely to attract long-term dwellers, especially retired people who make them their permanent homes. Younger people are less favorably inclined toward dachas—the lack of indoor plumbing and telephones, plus the hard work connected with gardening, no doubt play a role.

The gardens around dachas are a significant source of food to supplement what can be obtained in the city. During the summer, tomatoes, cucumbers, zucchini, onions, garlic, lettuce, all kinds of herbs, and early potatoes add to the variety of food available in the stores. In the fall, potatoes, cabbage, carrots, and onions are stored in cool storage places, pickled, or otherwise preserved. Home canning adds considerably to the winter diet.

Dachas are also a source of fruits and berries, even in very cold areas. Usually around each dacha grow apple trees, plum trees, and sometimes pear or cherry trees. Strawberries are very popular in early summer, gooseberries, black and red currants, and raspberries in midsummer, and "oble*pi*kha"/облегѝха " (orange buckthorn berries) in late summer. In autumn, mountain ash berries are popular.

Russians differentiate between a garden where vegetables and berries grow, an "ogo*rod*"/**огорóд**, and one primarily dedicated to flowers and trees, a "sad"/**сад**. If the garden contains both vegetables and flowers, "sad"/**сад** is used.

# 18. DATING, MARRIAGE, AND DIVORCE

Only in recent years has limited dating started in Russian high schools. Generally, youngsters rarely date until they reach age 16. During the last two years of high school, life is filled with studies and preparation for college exams. Moreover, any public display of affection between a male and a female student is likely to land the Romeo and Juliet in the principal's office. However, students attending the less academically demanding vocational and technical schools become romantically involved more readily. Nevertheless, while still in school, youngsters generally do things in groups, such as go to films, gather for parties at home, stroll in parks, or meet at the entrances to apartment buildings.

Real dating begins in college. The verb used for "going out" is "vstre*chat*sya"/**встреча́ться**, which literally means "to meet." Students gather at dances usually organized by the university's social club. Sometimes these dances are preceded by a film or some other kind of presentation such as a lecture. Working-class youth meet at events organized by clubs connected with factories. City-sponsored discotheques are also popular. Another popular meeting place is the movie theater. Likewise, each town, or each region in cities, has a special street, informally understood to be "the street of strolling." Here youngsters gather: pairs of girls walk arm-in-arm, boys in noisy groups gather around them—and friendships and romances begin.

In contrast to dating in Europe and the United States where young people can readily gather in inexpensive, convenient restaurants or cafés, in Russia there are very few such places. Diners in a Russian restaurant are expected to order a full dinner, with wine and vodka—something young people generally cannot afford.

Russians must be 18 years old to get married. Usually after a young person starts earning money, nothing can stop him or her from marrying. The typical age for young men to marry is anywhere from 22 to 26; for girls it is two or three years earlier. Recent statistics indicate that there is a tendency for girls to get married at an even younger age, at 17 or 18.

A couple must obtain a wedding certificate. The waiting period for this certificate is three months, but the waiting period is considerably reduced if the bride is pregnant. Wedding certificates are obtained from ZAGS, "(Ot*del*) *z*api si *a*ktov grazh*dan*skovo sosto*ya*niya," Civil Registry Office (**Отдѐл зап́иси а́ктов гражда́нского состоя́ния**), or in special Wedding Palaces, "Dvor*tsy* brakosoche*ta*niya"/**Дворцы́ бракосочета́ния**. Prior to the 1990s, most Russians were married in such Wedding Palaces. Since then there has been an increase in the number of weddings taking place in churches. The Russian Orthodox wedding ceremony is known for the special wedding crowns that are held above the bride's and groom's heads, as was described in the wedding of Levin and Kitty in Leo Tolstoy's *Anna Karenina*.

After the official wedding ceremony, the couple traditionally visits historically significant places, where they leave bouquets of flowers. In Moscow, the most popular choices are the Grave of the Unknown Soldier near the Kremlin and Sparrow Hills near Moscow State University with its impressive view of Moscow. In St. Petersburg, married couples can be seen at the Rostral Columns by the spit of Vasilevsky Island, the statue of the Bronze Horseman (Peter the Great), the Field of Mars, and Piskaryovskoe Memorial Cemetery. The newlyweds ride in a car with big wedding rings on the roof, a doll on the front of the hood, and decorations of flowers, ribbons, and balloons.

A wedding feast concludes the day's festivities. This feast takes place in an apartment, a restaurant, or in special banquet halls. Guests sit at tables laden with the best that the parents of the groom and the bride can afford (the two families share the expenses). Prior to eating, the groom's father toasts the couple. Appetizers and numerous meat and fish dishes are set on the tables or offered by servers to the guests. During the meal, many toasts are made. Frequent shouts of "*gor*ko," bitter (**го́рько**) can be heard, which is a signal that the groom should kiss the bride to "sweeten" life. Russians love music and singing, and songs resound throughout the celebration.

After the wedding, if a room can be found for them to squeeze into, the young couple typically will move in with one of the parents, due to a shortage of apartments. Only in the mid-1990s have some apartments become available in cities for rent or purchase. However, they are frightfully expensive and it is unusual for a young couple to be able to afford one of their own.

The divorce rate in Russia is very high, 30% (almost as high as in the United States), and it is rising. Statistics published in Russian newspapers indicate that from 1990 to 1992 the divorce rate increased by 15%. The reasons for the high rate are numerous: lack of privacy because of the housing shortage, alcoholism, personality and cultural differences, sexual incompatibility, and adultery.

# 19. "DO YOU NOT KNOW?"

The Russian way of asking a question is, instead of saying, "Please tell me where the Mariinsky Theater is located," to ask, "Do you not know where the Mariinsky Theater is located?" If the person responding to the question is an out-of-towner, unfamiliar with St. Petersburg's theaters, or unaware that the Kirov Theater has re-verted back to its original name, the Mariinsky—having the question posed in the negative makes it easier to answer "No, I do not" and not feel guilty about it.

# 20. EDUCATION AND UPBRINGING, *OBRAZOVANIYE* AND *VOSPITANIYE* (*ОБРАЗОВÁНИЕ* AND *ВОСПИТÁНИЕ*)

The Soviet government designed its educational policies to make sure that a person received not just an education, "obrazo*va*niye"/ **образовáние**, at school, but also "vospi*ta*niye"/**воспитáние**—moral upbringing and good breeding. Guided by the ideology of Marxism-Leninism, schools expected students not only to get good grades, but to be active members of the Young Octobrist, Pioneer, and Komsomol organizations (see Point 39, "Milestones"), wear their uniforms, love Lenin, the Motherland, and hate the Soviet Union's enemies. World War II was to be remembered and the school area's war veterans to be honored at school events. Great effort was exerted to instill in the students a love for physical labor. On the Saturday "su*bbot*nik"/**суббóтник** before Lenin's birthday (April 22), youngsters in cities were supposed to volunteer their time, helping with clean-up projects and aiding recycling efforts. In rural areas, schoolchildren helped with agricultural chores on collective farms (kolkhozes). Respect for teachers (elders in general), discipline, and the needs of the collective (as opposed to the individual) were stressed.

School always starts on September 1, unless that date falls on a Sunday, in which case opening day is September 2. Children enter the first grade at age 6 and generally attend school until they have completed the eleventh grade, although only nine grades are compulsory. Students generally walk to the neighborhood school. Elementary, middle-, and high-school students study together in one, multistoried building rather than in separate buildings as is common in American schools. From the first day of first grade, students are assigned to a homeroom that they will keep through the eleventh grade. Schools in populated, newer areas of the country sometimes have as many as six or seven homerooms per grade level. Students are divided into homerooms, or classes, of

30–40 students. Each homeroom receives its own letter (in Cyrillic, of course), 1A, 1B, and so forth. There is mingling among homerooms, but real closeness exists among the students within one homeroom. In a society in which not *what* you know but *who* you know is of prime importance, the friendships forged "na stu*dyen*cheskoy"/"u*chyo*noy ska*mye*," at a student desk (**на студéнческой/учёной скамьé**) cannot be overestimated.

A system of special schools, "spetsi*al*niye *shk*oly"/"spets*shk*oly" (**специáльные шкóлы** or **спецшкóлы**), exists for economics, mathematics, art, or foreign languages. It may take students more than an hour to reach one of these schools. A student who attends a special English school will begin studying English daily in the second grade in groups of 10 to 15 students. By the end of the eleventh grade he or she will be nearly proficient in the language.

After the ninth grade, students may leave their general secondary school to complete the last two years in a vocational-technical school, where emphasis is on preparing students for skilled or semiskilled jobs in industry, agriculture, or office work.

Prior to the early 1990s even students not enrolled in a vocational-technical school, but in a general secondary or a special school, were required during their last two years to spend one day a week learning a skill such as sewing, house painting, or meat cutting.

Classes generally begin at 8:30 a.m. and last until 1:30 or 2:30 p.m., six days a week. However, in the late 1980s, many schools started a five-day week, citing parental pressure to give children, especially in the early grades, a two-day weekend. In some localities, because of a lack of school buildings, students attend school in two shifts; the second group begins classes around 1:30 p.m. and ends at 6:30 or 7:00 p.m.

The 1990s have seen other changes in secondary education. Whereas school formerly was compulsory, free, and coeducational, some private schools "*cha*stniye *shk*oly," "gim*naz*ii," or "li*tsye*i" (**чáстные шкóлы, гимнáзии**, or **лицéи** ) now charge for education and limit enrollment to only girls or only boys. Education remains compulsory until age fifteen. Private schools offer a wider curriculum than that found in state schools and hire the best teachers available, including native speakers for foreign languages. Church schools, illegal since the Bolshevik Revolution, are reappearing.

Until recently, courses for high school and college students were prescribed, with few electives allowed. The curriculum was set centrally for the entire country. In theory a student in a ninth-grade chemistry class could leave Moscow on a Friday, move to Irkutsk in Siberia over the weekend, and on Monday attend school in that city knowing what would be covered in class that day. In practice, of course, some variation existed in when the material was covered.

In Russian schools rote memorization plays a more significant role in the educational process than in the West. A delightful result of this practice are the many poems that Russians can recite by memory. Students too frequently, however, were expected merely to write down and retell what they heard in lectures. Since the 1990s, however, the ability to discuss and analyze has become more important. Teaching and testing in Russian schools and colleges is more frequently oral rather than written, in contrast to Western practice. The whispering of answers and the use of crib sheets is not considered to be the moral transgression that it is in American culture. This whispering is a bonding experience among friends and a vote against authority.

To be admitted into an institution of higher learning, or a "VUZ"/**ВУЗ**, a Russian youngster must take both a written and an oral examination during the summer after graduation. The importance of this test can best be appreciated if one realizes that the application process does not include letters of recommendation from teachers, high school grade point average, standardized test scores, or an applicant's essay. During their last year of high school students choose a profession, concentrate on the courses connected with that specialty to the exclusion of other courses, frequently study with a "repe*ti*tor," tutor (**репети́тор**), and try their hardest on the exam. Unlike the United States, where a student may apply to as many as ten colleges, a Russian student generally applies to only one. Competition for the best known institutions of higher learning is extremely stiff. Those who are not selected enter the work force (the importance of vocational training cannot be underestimated). Some students continue to pursue their goal of higher education by seeking admission to evening or extension courses.

When a "stu*dyent*," student (**студéнт**), is admitted to a "universi*tyet*," university (**университéт**), or an "insti*tut*," institute (**институ́т**), he or she becomes part of a group, much like the pupils in elementary through high school. The student has already chosen his or her speciality, hence most of the courses are compulsory, with few electives. Depending on the field of specialization, the years of study range from four to six. In the final year, the student must write and defend a thesis. Upon graduation, the degree earned is somewhat higher than a bachelor's degree.

Tuition is free at institutions of higher learning, and the majority of students tend to receive stipends. Medical care is free, rent for dormitories minimal, and cafeteria meals are subsidized by the government. Upon graduation, students are expected to work for two or three years in a government-assigned position.

After graduate study, or "aspiran*tura*" (**аспирантýра**), which generally lasts three years, graduates receive a "kandi*dat* na*uk*" (**кандидáт наýк**), or candidate of sciences degree, somewhat similar to a master's degree. (In the sciences it may actually be the equivalent of a master's degree.) Additional research and publication is required to be awarded a doctor of sciences, or a "*dok*tor na*uk*" (**дóктор наýк**), typically referred to as a "dokto*rat*" (**докторáт**). It is more difficult to obtain and more prestigious than an American Ph.D., requiring major original contributions to one's specialized area.

# 21. FAMILY

Traditionally in Russia, especially in the countryside, extended families lived together: grandparents, children, and grandchildren. Even now three generations live together under the same roof

20% of the time. Sometimes this is the result of the lack of apartments, sometimes it is the result of close family ties. Most of the time families try to obtain apartments in the same apartment complex or in close proximity to each other. Members of a family usually rely strongly on each other. People feel safe with their families, just as they do with truly close friends. The need for reliance on one's family played an especially strong role during the Stalin years, when denunciations to the KGB (see Point 29, "GULAG") to obtain a better apartment or a desired job, for example, were common practice. The outcome was distrust of anyone other than one's nearest and dearest. The closeness and warmth of so many Russian families has been commented on by visitors who have been able to penetrate beyond the "tourist" level during their stay in Russia.

The typical Russian family consists of four people: a "muzh," husband (**муж**), "zhe*na*," wife (**жена́**), and two children, a "doch/*doch*ka," daughter (**дочь/до́чка** ), and/or a "syn," son (**сын** ), and may include grandparents if they are still living: a "*de*dushka," grandfather (**де́душка**), and a "*ba*bushka," grandmother (**ба́бушка**). The terms for brother and sister are "brat"/**брат** and "ses*tra*"/ **сестра́**. Cousins are also frequently referred to as "brat"/**брат** and "ses*tra*"/**сестра́**, instead of the formal names "dvo*yu*rodniy brat"/ **двою́родный брат** and "dvo*yu*rodnaya ses*tra*"/**двою́родная сестра́**. This is especially common if one is an only child and does not have a brother or a sister. To indicate that "brat"/**брат** and ses*tra*"/ **сестра́** refer to one's real brother or sister, "rod*noy* brat"/**родно́й брат** and "rod*na*ya ses*tra*"/**родна́я сестра́** are used.

During the Soviet period most women worked outside the home. Although there were exceptions, women also did the majority of work connected with maintaining a home and a family— shopping, cooking, cleaning, and taking care of the children. There seems to be a movement among the younger generation for men to be more helpful in a family setting.

## 22. FIBBING, *VRANYO (ВРАНЬЁ)*

Every culture has a different attitude and explanation for a fib, or a "white lie," which in Russian is referred to as "vran*yo*"/**враньё**. One uses it to be polite, nice, and in order not to offend another person or say anything that would cause problems. Russians do not want to embarrass or disappoint guests. Visitors should be especially aware of this Russian trait.

## 23. FLOWERS

Flowers have always played a large role in Russian social life. They are presented to visitors and relatives as they arrive or leave. When going to someone's house as a guest, flowers are almost obligatory. Be aware of traditional associations connected with flowers. For example, flowers in even numbers are appropriate only for funerals; uneven numbers are offered in other situations. The colors of flowers also have connotations: white—innocence, red—love, yellow—sadness and betrayal. Generally roses are not given to men, gladioluses are. Carnations are traditionally associated with the Bolshevik Revolution, and on November 7th carnations were frequently given to veterans of the 1917 Revolution and World War II.

In the 1980s, the flower industry became one of the first private enterprises. In large cities flowers are now sold the whole year round—at the metro and train stations, at underground street crossings, and in front of large stores and cemeteries. The most popular flowers are carnations and roses. In the spring one can find tulips, irises, and daffodils; in the summer there are peonies, daisies, and gladioluses. Fall finds dahlias and chrysanthemums being sold. In addition to the flowers grown in hothouses or in individual gardens, Russians are very fond of flowers found in the fields and forests: lilies of the valley, forget-me-nots, and field daisies. Russians also love flowering bushes, especially lilacs, jasmine (similar to mock orange), and trees like the bird cherry.

# 24. FOREIGNERS

Russians have an ambivalent attitude toward foreigners. During the reign of Peter the Great (1682–1725), credited with opening a "window to Europe," representatives of six countries served in Russia. Foreigners were invited to Russia as soldiers and generals to serve in the military, as engineers and architects to build new cities, as scientists and doctors to develop science and medicine, as scholars to teach in schools and tutor in private households, and as artists to entertain the nobility. Many Russians considered anything foreign to be superior. Foreign goods were sought and foreign literature was imitated. For many decades during the nineteenth century the Russian nobility strove to live like the French nobility—they spoke French at home, wore French fashions, and built and decorated their homes in the French manner. French was the first language of Aleksander Pushkin, Russia's most beloved poet. Pushkin's Russian peasant nanny was the one who taught him Russian.

There were those in Russian society, however, who resented this bowing to the West. In the nineteenth century two camps formed: Westernizers and Slavophiles. The former, of which Ivan Turgenev was an adherent, felt that Russia as a part of Europe should follow the European model in its development, rationalism, and materialism. Slavophiles felt that Russia had its own destiny, and that Russia's strength lay in the Orthodox Church, autocracy, and the peasant communes. These two divergent outlooks on the West and Russia's roots are still influential in present-day Russian intellectual thought and political life. Mikhail Gorbachev and Boris Yeltsin belong to the Westernizer tradition; the conservative writers Valentin Rasputin and Aleksander Solzhenitsyn are part of the Slavophile tradition.

Nothwithstanding the adulation frequently shown to everything foreign, a negative attitude toward foreigners also exists. Xenophobia is reflected in the negative way foreigners are presented in Russian opera (e.g., *The Tsar's Bride*), in Russian literature, and in the attitude that they can (should) be taken advantage of in financial transactions. During Stalin's time, any evidence of interest in and respect toward Western intellectual thought, art, or fashion could cost the offender his or her life.

In the 1990s this admiration and fear continues to exist in Russian society. On the one hand foreigners are sought out for the Western currency they possess. But on the other hand, there is resentment of the fact that there are doors open to them because of their currency which are closed to the typical Russian. In the business sphere, foreigners are invited to invest in Russia through ads in newspapers and magazines; however, their legal rights remain in flux. Pro-Western views are likely to be held by younger, well-educated people studying or working in big cities in the fields of economics, computer science, or any advanced disciplines. People living in the provinces, war veterans, and working people are more likely to be anti-Western.

English-speaking foreigners who wish to live in the larger cities in Russia will find that in the early 1990s, a nascent service industry caters to them. Three newspapers are published in English, a radio station broadcasts in English, and CNN can be received in many apartments and hotels. Some "poli*kli*niki," clinics (**поликли́ники**), cater only to those with hard currency, as do many taxi drivers. The danger of such an "all-English world" for foreigners who choose not to be involved with the Russian world is possible isolation from the country and its citizens.

# 25. FRIEND, *DRUG ["DROOG"] (ДРУГ)*, AND WAYS TO DENOTE FRIENDSHIP

The Russian language has a number of words for "friend." However, there are significant differences in meaning, depending on the closeness of the relationship. An acquaintance is a "*znako*miy" **знако́мый**. "Pri*ya*tel"/**Прия́тель** is the term for people with whom one has a closer relationships. The closest relationships are expressed by the terms "drug" [pronounced "droog"], friend, male or female (**друг**), and "po*dru*ga," female friend (**подру́га**). One feels blessed to have three or four such friends. For a Russian, having a close friend carries a significantly more important role than for those in most other countries. In times of difficulties and hostility under the tsars and the dictators, a devoted friend, who could be truly trusted and from whom one could receive support and understanding, was a genuine treasure. Such friends can be called on the telephone at any time during the day or night, money can be borrowed from them, and a telephone call is not required before a house visit.

The terms "boyfriend" and "girlfriend" do not exist in Russian. In a dating situation, the words "molo*doy* chelo*vyek*"/**молодо́й челове́к**, and "*pa*ren"/**па́рень** are used for boyfriend, and "*dye*vushka"/**де́вушка** for girlfriend. If a live-in boyfriend or girlfriend is involved, the adjective "neras*pi*sanniy," officially not registered, i.e., not married (**нераспи́санный**), will be added. "Lyu*bov*nik"/**любо́вник** and "so*zhi*tel"/**сожи́тель** are two additional terms for "lover." Until the 1990s, live-in situations occurred considerably less frequently than in the West, primarily due to the lack of available apartments. Lately, as apartments have become more available for rent or purchase, there is an increase in such live-in situations for those who have money.

# 26. GESTURES

Russians as a people are not as demonstrative with gestures as some other European peoples. They tend to be similar to Americans. Moreover, many gestures, such as twirling a finger at one's temple to indicate that a person is crazy, rubbing three fingers together to convey the idea of a need for money, or holding up a thumb as a sign of approval, are the same for Russians and Americans. A certain number of signs do exist, of course, which are not common to both countries. Only recently have Russians begun to understand and use the Western sign for victory, i.e., two fingers held up like a "V." Likewise, as Russian films become more prevalent in the West, one sees the gesture that indicates the desire to have a drink, i.e., the flipping of fingers against the lower part of the jaw.

# 27. GIFTS

Russians, as a rule, are very generous people. The old adage is that if you compliment a Russian on an item he or she is wearing or has in the apartment, that item is likely to be given to you. Russians like to give gifts—and to receive them. Gifts are given on birthdays and on name days, on holidays such as International Women's Day (see Point 11, "Celebrations and Holidays"), on New Year's Day, and for the birth of a child, and graduations. Wedding and housewarming presents are usually the most generous.

The most popular gift is flowers, but Russians also give and like to receive books, especially literature and illustrated art books, records, audio and video cassettes (both blank and recorded), chocolates, jewelry, clothing (tee shirts, sweaters), shoes (especially sports shoes), electronic products, musical instruments, toys, and watches. More often than in the West, presents tend to be practical because of the difficult economic conditions in much of Russia. Practical gifts are especially popular for weddings and housewarmings.

Foreign visitors who are invited to a Russian house will always delight a hostess by presenting her with flowers as well as with books, liquor, candy, cosmetics, fancy soaps, items embellished with a school, company, city, or state logo, or toys if there are children in the house. Russians invariably bring a small gift (a toy, pen, crayon, or notebook) when visiting a house with a child. The gift should be offered immediately upon arrival.

Presents in Russia tend not to be gift wrapped, partly due to the lack of necessary materials. Also the gift frequently is not opened in the giver's presence. Some Russians feel that opening a gift immediately is a sign of inappropriate eagerness. If immediately opened, visitors may be surprised by a lack of gushing thanks for their gift and, if the gift is not opened upon receipt, no thanks may ever be received.

## 28. GREETINGS, SALUTATIONS, AND LEAVE-TAKINGS

In place of the ubiquitous American "hello," Russians have about five expressions that are appropriate at different times. "*Zdrav*stvuyte"/**здра́вствуйте** can be used at any time of the day. So can the expression "pri*vyét*"/**приве́т**, when addressing close acquaintances (those on an even social level with the person offering the greeting). Greetings related to a particular time of the day are "*do*broye *ut*ro," good morning (**до́брое у́тро**), "*do*briy dyen," good day (**до́брый день),** and "*do*briy *vye*cher," good evening (**до́брый ве́чер**). They can be said to anyone, i.e., close friends as well as superiors.

In the United States we tend to say "hello" to people even upon a second or third encounter within the same day. Russians, however, will merely nod their head, or smile, or say "pri*vyet*"/**привéт**. They will not repeat the word "*zdrav*stvuyte"/**здрáвствуйте** unless in frequent contact with foreign visitors.

After greeting someone, Russians frequently shake hands, and ask how you are doing. Most frequently this will be expressed by: "Kak de*la*"/**Как делá? The English equivalent is "How are you?" In American culture the answer is frequently ignored, because the question is considered to be a greeting which does not require an answer. However, Russians expect an answer to this question. The most frequent answers from a Russian will be "nor*mal*no"/**нормáльно** or "niche*vo*"/**ничегó**, which literally mean "normal" and "nothing"—best translated as "not too bad." Knowing that the answer will be one of these two words, some Russians greet each other by asking "How is your 'normal' (or 'nothing') doing?"

When leaving someone, "do svi*da*niya," until we meet again (**до свидáния**), is the most frequently used farewell. Young people and friends will use the term "po*ka*," so long (**покá**), "vse*vo*kho*ro*shevo"/**всегó хорóшего**, "vse*vo do*brovo"/**всегó дóброго** (all the best), or, very informally, simply "*do*brovo," literally "good" (**дóброго**). However, if the period of separation will be long, only "do svi*da*niya"/**до свидáния** is appropriate. If one does not expect to see a person again during one's lifetime, "farewell," "pro*shcha*yte"/**прощáйте** is said. It literally means "forgive me." "Spo*koi*noy *no*chi"/**спокóйной нóчи** is used to say goodnight to someone in the evening.

Russians and Americans differ in the way they leave a social gathering before it has ended. The Americans leave trying not to call attention to their early departure. Russians have a term for this: "ukho*dit* po-ameri*kan*ski"/**уходи́ть по-америкáнски**—to leave like an American. Others say "ukho*dit* po-an*gli*ski"/**уходи́ть по-англи́йски**—to leave like an Englishman. A Russian, in contrast, will acknowledge that an early departure is taking place.

# 29. GULAG (PRISON, EXILE), THE SECRET POLICE, AND THE KGB

The state security system, or the modern-day KGB, was instituted in the sixteenth century by Tsar Ivan the Terrible. In his struggles with the boyars (prominent members of the nobility), Ivan created the "oprichniki," who could destroy or exile a whole family. This police force, known as the "secret police" or the "third section," continued throughout the tsarist period. Those who ran afoul of the government could be executed, exiled, or sent to forced labor camps, "*ka*torga"/**ка́торга**, followed by a period of exile or "s*sy*lka"/**ссы́лка** from the capital. Fyodor Dostoevsky, considered—along with Leo Tolstoy—to be the foremost Russian writer of the nineteenth century, was arrested in 1849 for belonging to a radical political group. He spent four years in a labor camp, followed by six years in exile in the provinces, before being allowed to return to St. Petersburg (then the capital of Russia).

After the Bolshevik Revolution, the new leaders needed a state organization to suppress those opposed to the ideals of the Bolsheviks. "Kto ne s *na*mi, tot *pro*tiv nas." "Those who are not with us are against us." (**«Кто не с на́ми, тот про́тив нас.»**) The organization formed to fulfill the need became known as the KGB. The acronym comes from the first letters of the phrase "Komit*ye*t gosu*dar*stevnnoy bezo*pas*nosti," Committee for State Security (**Комите́т госуда́рственной безопа́сности**). Its members, like those who had worked for the tsarist secret police, were professionally respected. In 1991 their numbers were said to be about six million. They were aided and abetted by millions of informers, who either willingly or as a result of threats informed on the rest of the population—hence the distrust of anyone but one's closest friends or family members, the distrust of the telephone, the fear of public denunciations, and until recently the unwillingness to have anything to do with foreigners.

Those judged to be enemies of the people by the secret police under Communism in the early years after the Bolshevik Revolution included former aristocrats and tsarist army officers, and then later, rich peasants, or kulaks, members of the intelligentsia, or anyone who stood in the way of Stalin as he consolidated power after Lenin's death. The years 1936 and 1937, known as the years of "the purges" or the "Great Terror," are especially notorious for the number of arrests and executions carried out by the secret police. Those not executed were sent to concentration camps to labor in the building of canals, power stations, factories, or to work in mines—all under the harshest of conditions.

After Stalin's death in 1953, the KGB became somewhat less active. Premier Nikita Khrushchev, in a closed session to the Twentieth Party Congress on February 20, 1956, delivered what has become known as "the secret speech" or the "de-Stalinization speech," in which he described the mass terror exercised by the KGB against the Soviet peoples. Rehabilitated former prisoners began to appear in society with tales of horror. Literary works written "for the drawer" began to circulate in unofficial samizdat editions, and some of these works were eventually published before Khrushchev was ousted from power. Anna Akhmatova's poem *Requiem*, written during the years of 1935–1940, related her own personal anguish, as she stood in endless lines attempting to determine the fate of her arrested son. The work was not published in Russia until the late 1980s, after the advent of Gorbachev's glasnost.

The work of author Aleksander Solzhenitsyn, however, is most associated with this period in Russian history. Solzhenitsyn was arrested in 1945 after counterintelligence agents read a letter written by him to a friend, in which he obliquely disparaged Stalin. He was imprisoned for eight years. His experiences in prison provided Solzhenitsyn with the material for his novels. *One Day in the Life of Ivan Denisovich* appeared in 1962, after Khrushchev's intervention. For over two decades it was the major source of information about concentration camp experience.

With Khrushchev's ouster the brief literary thaw came to an end. Authors including Solzhenitsyn again wrote "for the drawer." Two of his later works, *The Cancer Ward* and *The First Circle*, were forerunners to the monumental work that gave the whole prison experience its title, *The Gulag Archipelago*—a survey of the Soviet system of forced labor, using the author's own reminiscences and other documentary evidence. The word "gulag" comes from the Russian for Main Administration of Prisons, "*Glav*noye *u*prav*lye*nie *lage*rey"/**Гла́вное управле́ние лагере́й**. Solzhenitsyn's last three works were refused publication in Russia and were published instead in the West. The appearance of the first volume of *The Gulag Archipelago* in Paris in 1973 caused an uproar in the Soviet Union and led to Solzhenitsyn's arrest and deportation.

In 1991 the KGB was replaced by the "Minis*tyer*stvo bezo*pas*nosti," Russian Security Ministry (**Министе́рство безопа́сности**), which in turn was replaced in 1993 by the "Fede*ral*naya *sluzh*ba kontrra*zvye*dki," Federal Counterintelligence Service (**Федера́льная слу́жба контрразве́дки**).

Every Soviet family suffered in some way during the years of Stalin's terror; millions were affected. Nevertheless, Stalin's crimes are not talked about that much in Russia today. Some people— especially those who believe in the need for a "strong man" (see Point 61) to lead Russia—even think that what happened was appropriate.

# 30. HEALTH CARE

The Russian health care system is in a somewhat uncertain state at present. Until 1987 the state system predominated. All medical care (except for prescription drugs bought at pharmacies) was free. Although on occasion excellent medical care was administered, there were many inadequacies in the system, such as inadequate medical equipment and scarcity of prescription drugs. After 1987 the first medical co-ops emerged. There also exist so-called private ("self-financing") clinics, "khozras*chot*niye poli*kli*niki"/

**хозрасчётные поликли́ники,** where patients are charged for dental, ophthalmological, homeophathic, or general therapeutic treatment. In the early 1990s, in order to improve medical care, various insurance systems were being examined.

The main illnesses that beset Russians are the common cold and the flu. The latter frequently sweeps a city as an epidemic. Although Russians believe that viruses spread colds, both doctors and patients believe that drafts, cold drinks, or sitting on cold surfaces such as floors or benches are also significant causes of colds. Russians who have a cold will not drink anything out of the refrigerator.

In 1990 the death rate surpassed the birth rate, and was higher for males. The leading cause of death is cardiovascular disease, followed by cancer. The "third disease," as it is frequently referred to in Russia, is alcoholism.

With one exception there is no restriction on how many days a Russian may be sick and absent from work. The one exception is if a Russian is sick three months in a row. Then he or she is expected to obtain a "*vre*mennaya inva*lid*nost," temporary disability (**вре́менная инвали́дность**). Since the worker on medical leave does not receive a regular salary but a reduced one similar to a pension, most people try to avoid this status. They return to work for a while and then take off again, thus continuing to draw a regular salary.

The health-consciousness of Americans who watch their fat intake and routinely check their cholesterol count has not spread to Russia. Salt consumption is a less serious problem, since Russian food tends to be more bland than spicy. Checks for diabetes do take place.

Most foreigners who visit Russia comment on the extensive smoking in public places. The idea of "non-smoking areas" has not yet reached Russia.

# 31. HOUSING AND HOUSES

The bigger cities of Russia look very similar. Except for the historical central areas, Russian cities and towns share a similar skyline: block after block of tall apartment buildings. World War II destroyed 89% of the housing in areas of Russia occupied by the German army. After the war, the Russian government made a colossal effort to replace destroyed houses, to raze housing with no modern conveniences, and to build new housing for citizens who wished to move to the cities.

The Stalin era in Moscow is known for its seven "wedding cake" buildings (four government offices, a hotel, apartments, and Moscow State University). In the Khrushchev era (1953–1964), the buildings tended to be five-storied, since buildings with more than five stories were required to have an elevator. The size of these apartments was rather small, and the ceilings were low. The goal was to build as many such apartments as possible to help the population. The buildings were expected to be torn down in 20 years; most of them, however, are still standing today.

In the Brezhnev era (1964–1982), the buildings typically had 9 to 12 stories and extended an entire block. Later, 14 to 18 stories per building were common. Buildings are usually made of concrete, prefabricated, and assembled on–site. Colorfully painted balconies add diversity to the buildings and to the city. Russians who travel to Europe and the United States invariably comment on the number of one- and two-story buildings found in cities there. Ilf and Petrov, two Russians writers who visited the United States in 1935, gave their travel memoirs the title "*Odnoetazhnaya Amerika,*" *One-Storied America* (*Одноэтáжная Амéрика*).

Most Russians in cities live in apartments which prior to the early 1960s belonged to the government. Each person was limited to 10.8 square yards of living space. In the 1990s this allotment was increased to 14.4 square yards, and some professionals were allowed an extra space of up to 21.2 square yards. The rent was minimal. A family of four (husband, wife, and two children) would typically have a two-room apartment, consisting of one room that served as a living/dining/bedroom for the parents and another room for the children. In addition, there would be areas not included in the two-room count: an entry area of some sort, a kitchen, and a "two-part" bathroom. In one little room would be a basin and a bathtub or shower and in another little room, the toilet. After 1962, Russians could purchase apartments in cooperative housing units. The individual rooms were larger, and the "so many meters per person" rule was not strictly enforced. Some cooperative apartment complexes have a "caretaker," similar to the French concierge, to help with maintenance and security. Repairs, such as those for electrical and plumbing problems, are free and are handled through an uprav*dom*, manager of a "block of flats" (**управдóм**).

Some Russians live in communal housing. As many as 10 to 18 families share a building. They have their own rooms, but all food preparation is done in one big kitchen. (The food is eaten in one's own apartment.) One or two bathrooms are shared by everyone. Individual meters (to measure water and electricity usage) for each family line the walls of the kitchen and the bathroom(s). Such housing is called "kommu*nal*ka"/**коммунáлка**, from "kommu*nal*naya kvar*ti*ra," communal apartment (**коммунáльная квартúра**).

Since the advent of perestroika, the influx of foreign businesses and their staffs have placed a premium on centrally located apartments. They are purchased by budding Russian capitalists, remodeled, and rented or sold to foreigners for offices or living quarters.

Upon entering an apartment or a dacha, a Russian will immediately remove his or her shoes or boots and put on "*ta*pochki," slippers (**тáпочки**), which are conveniently located near the entrance. When visiting others in informal situations, guests will be offered slippers by hosts. Although at formal events guests will wear their own shoes, they will wipe them carefully before entering an apartment.

The cold weather in much of Russia (see Point 65, "Temperature") and the warmth that Russians crave for their apartments has influenced the construction of buildings. Windows typically are double windows to more effectively keep out the cold. However, for purposes of ventilation, a small hinged windowpane, which can be opened separately from the window, is installed. This "*fort*ochka"/ **фóрточка** has been used by many a visitor to counter the heat in Russian apartments.

## 32. HYGIENE

Like many Europeans, Russians do not consider it essential to take daily showers or baths. Before the advent of bathrooms, the weekly trip to the *banya* (see Point 8, "Banya") served as the means to cleanliness, and a weekly bath is still not uncommon. This fact, plus a reluctance to dryclean or wash clothes (washing machines in Russian homes are still not common, and those that do exist are semi-automatic), often can lead to "fragrant" encounters. However, in recent years attitudes toward hygiene are changing. Deodorants are becoming more readily available and used. No matter how frequently Russians take a shower or bath, it is generally done prior to retiring for the night. Many Russians are most perplexed by the habit of daily washing of hair; some Russian doctors consider washing hair more than once a week bad for the hair.

## 33. ICE AND THE PURITY OF RUSSIAN WATER

As is true in much of Europe, Russians do not use ice cubes in their drinks. Drinks are generally offered at room temperature and without ice. Russians with a sore throat or sick with the flu will never drink anything refrigerated, much less anything that has an ice cube in it. Today in hotels that cater to tourists ice is available. But should it be used? There are Russian ecologists who consider one fourth of Russia's drinking water unsafe. The city of St. Petersburg, built on a swamp in the early eighteenth century, is well-known for its brownish-looking water, beset with the parasite *giardia lamblia*. One should not drink this water under any circumstances, but rather rely on bottled water. And remember, if water is to be avoided in a particular locality, so should ice.

# 34. THE INTELLIGENTSIA

In the nineteenth century the term intelligentsia referred to educated people who generally held radical left-wing views and acted on their consciences by criticizing the existing Russian order. Idealism characterized the intelligentsia. After the emancipation of the serfs in 1861, many members of the intelligentsia joined the group who came to be known as the Populists and went into the countryside to educate the freed serfs. After the revolution of 1917, the intelligentsia was considered unreliable and was discriminated against by the Bolsheviks; good jobs, admission to colleges, and memberships in the Communist Party were hard to obtain.

In the 1930s the Communist Party strove to create a new, loyal intelligentsia. In 1936 Stalin proclaimed that the intelligentsia was a stratum of society, "pro*sloy*ka"/**прослойка** [not a class], and that students, independent professional people, and nonmanual employees above the clerical level belonged to it. The intelligentsia was courted. Stalin labeled them "the engineers of human souls." Writers, artists, and composers who joined professional associations received privileges such as passes or "put*yov*ki"/**путёвки** for stays at a "Dom *tvor*chestva," House of Creativity (**Дом тво́рчества**), where they could work and/or vacation. The values of the intelligentsia were praised and the arts were subsidized.

With the demise of the Soviet Union, the intelligentsia became impoverished. The monetary support offered by the government to artistic endeavors largely vanished. As a result, many cultural undertakings ended. For example, subsidized journals such as *Soviet Film* ceased publication. The Western orientation of the arts and the new market economy hurt Russian artistic efforts. Businessmen took over the Houses of Creativity; they could afford to stay there, the intelligentsia could not. Many members of the intelligentsia left Russia for temporary jobs in the West or emigrated. Many of those who remain are eager to take advantage of the new freedoms to do creative work in their professions.

# 35. INTRODUCTIONS

Upon being introduced to a Russian, one usually shakes hands. In American culture in a social or business setting, it is considered important that introductions be made to people who are not acquainted with one another. This is not the case in Russia. You may be in a social or business setting with acquaintances when someone unknown joins you, and no attempt is made to introduce that person. Your choice is to remain silent and let the conversation go on without you, or take the initiative and introduce yourself.

# 36. IN THE KITCHEN

Just like in American homes, the kitchen seems to be the most popular room in Russian homes. Family members and close friends gather there to eat and chat. If you are invited into the kitchen for a meal, a cup of tea, or something stronger, consider it a compliment. It is in the kitchen that the most meaningful conversations take place between a visitor and a Russian. Russian love for discussion lasting long into the night is well-known. A visitor who has an opportunity to participate in this Russian experience is a lucky one indeed.

The table in a small Russian kitchen is generally surrounded by stools which are pushed under the table when not in use. By the sink is a place where dishes can dry after being washed. The shelf just above the sink is similarly intended for this purpose. The bottom shelf does not have a solid plank, but slots, so that dishes placed above it in a dish "caddy" can drip dry. Dishwashing liquid is found infrequently; instead, a dishcloth or a sponge is run across a bar of soap. Dishwashers are very rare. The gas stove has an oven and four burners ignited by a match or an electrical starter. Some families have two refrigerators and a freezer, sometimes located in a corridor. The extra refrigerator and the freezer are especially important for those who have a dacha and need a place to store pickled vegetables, preserves, and the meat of animals raised in the country. Russians frequently put food left over in a pot directly into the refrigerator. Due to the lack or shortage of wax paper, aluminum foil, or the like, generally no cover is placed on the pot.

# 37. LETTERS, GREETING CARDS, AND ANNOUNCEMENTS

Letter-writing is more prevalent in Russia than in the West. Distrust of the telephone may account partly for this fact. (See Point #64, "The Telephone.")

Envelopes in Russia are addressed in reverse order to those in the United States:

| zip code (index) | 121433 | **121433** |
| city and city region | Mosk*va* | **Москва́** |
| street name | P*ye*rviy  Akadem*ich*eski pro*ye*zd | **Пе́рвый Академи́ческий прое́зд** |
| building and apartment numbers | Dom 34/4, kv. 107 | **Дом 34/4, кв. 107** |
| addressee (in the dative case) | Ev*do*khinoy, *Li*lii Petro*v*ne | **Евдо́хиной, Ли́лии Петро́вне** |

Care must be exercised as to where the "To" and "From" information is written. The size of most Russian envelopes is $6\frac{1}{2}$" x $4\frac{1}{2}$". Many of these envelopes come already preprinted with the words "ku*da*," where (**куда́**), and "ko*my*," to whom (**кому́**). There is a special place on the envelope for the zip code; in order for sorting machines to read the numbers, they are written following a specific style illustrated on the envelope. When the envelopes are not preprinted, the "To" address is written one-quarter of the distance from the top and the left of the envelope. The "From" address is then written at the bottom quarter of the envelope. A thick black line separates the "To" and "From" parts of the envelope.

Centered on the right in personal letters one writes the address (optional) and date, and in official letters, the address and date.

## Personal letters

Salutations in personal letters are centered on the first line of the letter after the (optional) address and date:

| | | |
|---|---|---|
| Doro*goy* (moy) . . . , | (My) dear . . . [masculine] | Дорого́й (мой) . . . , |
| Doro*gaya* (mo*ya*) . . . , | (My) dear . . . [feminine] | Дорога́я (моя) . . . , |
| Doro*giye* (mo*i*) . . . , | (My) dear . . . [plural] | Дороги́е (мой) . . . , |
| Rod*noy* (nash) | (Our) own . . . [masculine] | Родно́й (наш) . . . |
| Rod*naya* (*na*sha) | (Our) own . . . [feminine] | Родна́я (на́ша) . . . |
| Rod*niye* (*na*shi) | (Our) own . . . [plural] | Родны́е (на́ши) . . . |
| *Zdravs*tvuyte (mo*i*) *mi*liye! | Greetings (my) dear ones! | Здра́вствуйте (мой) ми́лые! |
| Pri*vet* iz Chicago! | Hello from Chicago! | Приве́т из Чика́го! |

It is considered rude to begin a letter with the name of a person, i.e., "Marina!" without an endearing term in front of it, i.e., "Dear Marina."

Paragraphs are always indented ("*kras*naya stro*ka*"/кра́сная строка́) in Russian letters. Block style is not used.

## Closings in personal letters

| | | |
|---|---|---|
| S lyu*bov*yu, | With love, | С любо́вью, |
| Do svi*da*niya/ | Goodby/Until | До свида́ния/ |
| Do *vstre*chi, | we meet again, | До встре́чи, |
| Tse*lu*yu/ | I kiss you | Целу́ю/Обнима́ю, |
| Obni*ma*yu, | (Kisses . . . )/ | |
| | I embrace you, | |
| Vse*vo* kho*ro*shevo/ | All the best! | Всего́ хоро́шего/ |
| *do*brovo! | | до́брого! |
| Zhe*la*yu u*da*chi. | I wish you success. | Жела́ю уда́чи. |
| Zhdu ot*ve*ta. | I await (your) | Жду отве́та. |
| | answer. | |

## Business and other formal letters

Salutations in business and other formal letters are centered (as in personal letters) on the first line after the address and date. Typical salutations are:

| | | |
|---|---|---|
| Uva*zha*em-iy, -aya, -iye . . . , | Respected . . . , | Уважа́ем-ый, -ая, -ые . . . , |
| Mnogouva*zha*emiy, -aya, -iye . . . , | Much respected . . . , | Многоуважа́ем-ый, -ая, -ые . . . , |
| Glubokouva*zha*emiy, -aya, -iye . . . , | Deeply respected [masculine, feminine, plural endings] . . . , | Глубокоуважа́емый, -ая, -ые . . . , |
| Gospo*din*, gospo*zha*, gospo*da* . . . , | Mr., Miss or Mrs., Sirs . . . , | Господи́н, госпожа́, господа́ . . . , |

It is considered more polite to put an adjective such as "Respected" in front of "Mr.," rather than starting out a letter only with the latter.

## Closings in business and other formal letters

| | | |
|---|---|---|
| S uva*zhy*eniem, | Respectfully, | С уважéнием, |
| *I*skrenne, | Sincerely, | Искренне, |
| Za*ra*nee | In advance I | Зарáнее |
| blago*da*ren, | [masculine, | благодáрен, |
| blago*da*rna, | feminine, | благодáрна, |
| blago*da*rny | plural | благодáрны, |
| | adjectival | |
| | endings] | |
| | thank you, | |
| Za*ra*nee | In advance I | Зарáнее |
| blago*da*ryu, | thank you, | благодарю, |
| | [verb form] | |

Greeting cards are popular in Russia. People send cards to note birthdays, wedding anniversaries, and major holidays. New Year's Eve, International Women's Day, and Victory Day are the most popular occasions for sending cards. May Day cards and November 7th cards in particular have lost their importance in the 1990s, while Christmas and Easter cards have become increasingly popular. In addition there are cards to commemorate a baby's birth, a first paycheck, and for a housewarming. And just as we in the U. S. have our "Secretary's Day," Russians have "Builder's Day," "Teacher's Day," "Day Dedicated to the Medical Profession," and so forth.

# 38. MEALS AND MEALTIMES

The Russian day starts with a "*zav*trak," breakfast (**за́втрак**), in the morning, "o*byed*," dinner (**обе́д**), around 1:00—the main meal of the day, with appetizers, soup, a main dish, and a dessert—and "*uz*hin," supper (**у́жин**), around 7:00 p.m. or later, with appetizers, a main course, and possibly a dessert. The concept of "lunch" is generally unknown in Russia, although lately because of the large number of foreign visitors, the word is being heard and understood as something in between a breakfast and a Russian dinner. A "*pol*dnik," afternoon snack (**по́лдник**), around 4:00 p.m., is popular with children (after their naps) both at home and at schools, as well as with adults in sanatoriums or rest houses.

At breakfast, eggs, sausage, cold cuts, kasha, hot dogs, cheese, bread with butter, and tea or coffee are served. Hot cereals, especially oatmeal, are popular with mothers feeding school-age children. As of the early 1990s, cold cereals were not being produced in Russia and are currently available only in stores that sell foreign goods.

"*Zaku*ski," appetizers (**Заку́ски**), begin dinner, the main meal of the day. Frequently, they are the most interesting part of the dinner: caviar, pâté, pickles, cheese, smoked fish, herring, all kinds of mushrooms, marinated vegetables, and various kinds of "salads"—consisting of vegetables, potatoes, eggs, meat, or fish. It is easy to mistake the appetizers for the main meal. (It might be wise, if it can be done politely, to inquire what is on the menu at the start of a meal.) "*Pyer*voe"/**Пе́рвое** is a soup course, while "vto*roy*e"/**второ́е** includes meat or fish dishes, with an accompaniment of potatoes, rice or noodles, and fresh (when available) or marinated vegetables. "*Tre*tye"/**Тре́тье** is the dessert course, possibly including chocolates, cakes, and dishes such as "kom*pot*," stewed fruit (**компо́т**), or "*ki*sel," a type of fruit purée (**кисе́ль**).

The evening meal is a version of dinner without a soup course and sometimes without a dessert course. However in the countryside, where workers in the fields do not have soup with their noon meal, soup is eaten at the evening meal.

Tea is the most frequently served breakfast drink even for children. Drinking orange juice or the like is not a Russian tradition in the mornings. Mineral water or soft drinks may be offered during dinner and supper, and they will most likely be served at room temperature, as Russians generally do not use ice. For festive occasions, bottles of champagne, wine, vodka, or cognac may also be on the table. Tea or coffee, if available, will be offered at the end of the meal. (See Points 33, "Ice, and the Purity of Russian Drinking Water," 63, "Tea," and 71, "Vodka and Drinking.")

Russian cooking is one of the distinctive cuisines of the world, and the Russian table in a family setting is a feast for the eyes as well as the palate. Its most famous dishes are "ik*ra*," caviar (**икра́**), sturgeon's eggs (if black) and salmon eggs (if red), served with bread, pancakes, or potatoes; a beet-based soup, "borshch" (**борщ**), and a beef, mushroom, and sour cream sauce dish, beef stroganoff ("bef-*strog*anov"/**беф-стро́ганов**), created by a French chef for the Russian Count Stroganov. Russian pancakes, called "bli*ny*"/**блины́,** have saved many a working Russian hostess faced with unexpected guests and a bare cupboard. Pancakes, served with caviar (when available and affordable) or herring, sour cream, and jams, and accompanied by vodka, delight many a foreign visitor, as recounted by opera singer Galina Vishnevskaya (wife of the cellist and conductor Mstislav Rostropovich), before the couple was expelled from the former Soviet Union.

# 39. MILESTONES

A newborn Russian baby is unlikely to be baptized. In the late 1980s only one third of the Soviet population were believers in God, and half of those were Moslems. However, a baby born into a Russian Orthodox family is baptized within three months or so of birth by being immersed in water.

In all likelihood, both parents work, so a child is generally placed in a nursery or childcare center. Russian youngsters enter first grade at age 6. At age 16 a Russian receives an internal passport, indicating nationality and place of residence, and containing a photograph. However, full citizenship rights, including the right to vote, obtain a driver's license, and get married, are not granted until age 18. Graduation from high school, generally at 17 years of age, is marked by celebrating all night.

A Russian must be 18 to marry. Upon receipt of special permission girls may marry earlier than boys. Russians celebrate birthdays not in a restaurant or at dinner at a friend's house but by staying at home in the evening on their birthdays while relatives and friends drop by with congratulations. The person celebrating the birthday provides the food, not the guests. Likewise, should a celebration take place during the day in the workplace, the "birthday person" provides the food for the gathering. However, gifts are presented in the name of the entire work group.

Upon reaching the age of 18, all males are required to serve in the Russian military for two years. University students may receive a deferment.

Retirement age for a woman is 55 provided she has a 20-year record of work service, or "stazh"/стаж. Males retire at age 60, with 25 years of work service. When infirmity or serious ill health comes, only if there are no living children will a Russian retire to a nursing home ("*star*cheskiy dom" or "dom dlya prestar*ye*lykh"/ста́рческий дом or дом для престаре́лых). Nursing homes are extremely rare; the ones that exist are largely sponsored by organizations such as professional trade unions. The reputation of nursing homes is not very favorable.

When someone passes away, family and friends gather to bid farewell. This can take place at home or in the workplace. Frequently the gathering will be at the cemetery, where the body will be in an open casket. In Russian Orthodox families, the body lies in an open casket at home for a night, friends come to say farewell, and prayers are said throughout the night. The deceased may also be taken to the church, and a special funeral service, "otpe*va*niye"/

**отпева́ние**, accompanied by a choir, may take place.

There are no funeral homes of the kind we have in the U. S., but there are rooms next to cemeteries set aside for the viewing of the body. On the day of the burial farewell words are said, then the casket is closed and lowered into the ground. Each person throws a handful of earth onto the casket. Family and guests will then observe a wake, "po*min*ki"/**поми́нки**, generally in a private home, but occasionally in a private room at a restaurant, with eating and drinking.

If the body is laid out at home, by tradition, all the mirrors in the home of the deceased are covered until the ninth day, "de*vya*tiy dyen"/**девя́тый день**, after the death, at which time tradition says that the soul of the deceased departs the earth. Friends and family gather at this time, and there is eating and drinking. Forty days, "soroko*voy* dyen"/**сороково́й день**, after the death, family and friends again gather, visit the cemetery, and again share a rich table.

Milestones connected with the Communist party included admittance to "oktya*brya*ta"/**октября́та** (the Octobrists—from the month the 1917 Bolshevik Revolution took place) for youngsters ages 6 to 9, then to "pio*ne̒ry*"/**пионе́ры** (the Pioneers), for those ages 10 to 15, and then on to "komso*mol*tsy"/**комсомо́льцы** (the Komsomols), for those ages 14 to 28. These organizations were disbanded in 1991. Before 1991 acceptance into the Communist Party was considered to be a great honor and an occasion to celebrate; at that time 7–10% of the population were members of the Communist Party. In 1991 there were 19 million members of the Communist Party in what was then the Soviet Union.

# 40. MONETARY UNITS

The main monetary unit of Russia is the ruble, "rubl"/**рубль**. Until the early 1990s, the other monetary unit in circulation was the kopek, "ko*pey*ka"/**копéйка**, with one hundred kopeks equal to one ruble, just as one hundred pennies (cents) make a dollar. However, since the inflation of the early 1990s, kopeks are no longer used. The costs of goods have risen steadily. The cost of a metro ride, which in 1990 was five kopeks, rose to 50 kopeks in November 1992, and to 250 rubles in early 1994.

# 41. MUSHROOMS

In late summer and early fall there is no more popular sport in Russia than "gathering mushrooms" ("sobi*rat* gri*by*"/**собирáть грибы́**). Russians head for the woods loaded with empty baskets. From childhood they have accompanied their parents on such outings and have become thoroughly acquainted with where mushrooms are to be found and which mushrooms are edible. In the evening, people with loaded baskets return to the villages or board trains back to the big cities. Mushrooms that are not immediately enjoyed are preserved for later consumption. Pickled, marinated mushrooms appear at the table on festive occasions during the rest of the year. Russians do not eat mushrooms raw and are surprised to find raw mushrooms in tossed salads or around an appetizer dip, two "dishes" largely unknown to Russians.

# 42. *NEKULTURNO*, UNCULTURED (*НЕКУЛЬТУ́РНО*)

Countries and cultures have standards that they consider a minimum for behavior. Those who violate these standards are labeled "uncultured." The Soviet Union had a set list of actions that were considered unacceptable. (In the mid 1990s attitudes are changing slightly on the do's and don'ts of behavior.) Some examples of unacceptable behavior: not checking one's coat in the cloakroom (it is not permitted to take it into a theater or a restaurant), sitting on the floor in public buildings, putting one's feet on a chair in front of you, or for a man, sitting with one's legs sprawled out. Such actions frequently elicited the admonition "one may not/one should not"—nel*zya*/**нельзя**.

# 43. PATRONYMICS

Except within a family or among very close friends, Russians address each other by their first names "*im*ya"/**и́мя** (in full form, not a diminutive) and patronymics, or "*ot*chestvo" /**о́тчество**. When Russians are among foreign visitors this practice may be less prevalent.

To form a patronymic, a man adds the suffix "-ovich" ("-evich") [**-ович (-евич)**] to his father's first name I*van* + "-ovich" = "I*van* I*va*novich" (**Ива́н + -ович = Ива́н Ива́нович**), while a woman adds "-ovna" (-evna) [**-овна (-евна)**] to her father's first name Ivan + "-ovna" = "Ma*ri*na I*va*novna" (**Ива́н + -овна = Мари́на Ива́новна**).

Occasionally, among relatively close friends, or when wishing to show respect to someone with whom one is very close, Russians will address a person with only the patronymic, i.e., without the first name.

# 44. PEOPLE'S NAMES AND NAME DAYS

Some Russian first names have been popular for generations: there have always been many boys named "Volodya" (**Воло́дя**), "Ilya" (**Илья́**), "Sasha" (**Са́ша**), "Misha" (**Ми́ша**), "Andrey" (**Андре́й**), and Seryozha" (**Серёжа**); many girls have been called "Mariya" (**Мари́я**), "Natasha" (**Ната́ша**), "Galya" (**Га́ля**), "Tatyana" (**Татья́на**), or "Anna" (**Анна**). From time to time, other names have become fashionable. In the early Soviet period, some children received newly coined names such as "Vladilyena" or Ninyel" (**Владиле́на** or **Нине́л**)—to honor "Vladimir Lenin" (**Влади́мир Ле́нин**)—the latter name is Lenin spelled backwards— or even "Elecktrofikatsiya" (**Электрофика́ция**) or "Dneproges" (**Днепрогэ́с**)—to show enthusiastic support for the goal of complete electrification of the country or the building of a hydroelectric station on the Dnieper. Foreign names have also been popular at times, especially in the late 1930s before World War II: "Robert" (**Ро́берт**), "Margarita" (**Маргари́та**), "Mark" (**Марк**), "Eduard" (**Эдуа́рд**). In the 1990s, popular Russian male names are "Ivan" (**Ива́н**), "Boris" (**Бори́с**), and "Kirill" (**Кири́лл**), while for girls the popular names are "Ekaterina" (**Екатери́на**), "Anna" (**А́нна**), "Elizavyeta" (**Елизаве́та**).

The Russian word for "last name" is familiya/**фами́лия**, which must not be confused with the English word "family," "semya"/**семья́** in Russian. Common last names are: "Kuznetsov" (**Кузнецо́в**), "Ivanov" (**Ивано́в**), "Petrov" (**Петро́в**), "Sidorov" (**Си́доров**), "Smirnov" (**Смирно́в**), "Plotnikov" (**Пло́тников**), "Pavlov" (**Па́влов**), "Nikitin" (**Ники́тин**), and "Mikhaylov" (**Миха́йлов**). Frequently a last name is formed from a first name, e.g., "Ivanov" (**Ивано́в**) from "Ivan" (**Ива́н**), or from a profession, e.g., "Kuznetsov" (**Кузнецо́в**), from "(black)smith."

The gender of first names in their formal form can be determined from their endings. Most female names end in -a/-**a** or -ya/-**я**. "Natasha," "Galya" (**Ната́ша, Га́ля**); masculine names in a consonant, "Ivan," "Boris" (**Ива́н, Бори́с**). Female diminutives end in -a/**-a** and -ya/**-я**, "*I*ra," "*Ka*tya" (**Úра, Kа́тя**), and so do many male diminutives, "*Sa*sha," "*Bo*rya" (**Cа́ша, Бо́ря**). Masculine last names end in consonants, "Smir*nov*"/**Смирно́в**, feminine in -a/**-a** or -ya/**-я**, "Smir*nova*," "Kali*nov*skaya" (**Смирно́ва, Калино́вская**), and the plural form of last names ends -y/**-ы**, -i/**-и**, or -iye/**-ие** "Smir*novy*," "Kali*nov*skiye" (**Смирно́вы, Калино́вские**).

In addition to a first name, a patronymic, and a last name, those Russians who are members of the Russian Orthodox Church or (less frequently) are Roman Catholics also have a saint's name. Each day of the year, one or more saints are honored by these churches. Their names appear on church calendars. When parents choose a name for a child, the day the church honors a saint by that name becomes the child's name day. Prior to the 1917 revolution, name days were celebrated more frequently with friends than were birthdays. From the calendar, everyone knew a friend's name day and would visit the friend on that day. The party for Tatyana in Alexander Pushkin's *Eugene Onegin* (and Tchaikovsky's opera of the same name) is held on her name day, not on her birthday.

# 45. PHYSICAL DISTANCE AND CONTACT

As in other European countries such as Spain, Russians do not require the physical distance between two speakers that American culture demands. For them a distance of 12 inches is quite normal; hence while conversing a Russian is likely to stand closer to his or her speaking companion than an American. The same is true for people waiting in line, eating in a restaurant, or sitting on park benches. In crowded city transport, especially during rush hours, people are frequently packed like sardines, resulting in considerable unavoidable shoving and pushing. This situation does not lead to the flaring of tempers, though those boarding or exiting buses too slowly may get chastised for their slowness.

Russians have physical contact with each other in their daily lives more frequently than we do in the United States. On the street, girls, women, and couples may stroll arm in arm. People shake hands readily. Upon meeting an acquaintance, especially one they have not seen for a while, some Russian men are likely to embrace and kiss that person on the cheek (sometimes three times, alternating cheeks). Occasionally, the kiss may even be on the lips. There are many men, however, who limit their greetings to a handshake or a clap on the shoulder. Touching the person one is conversing with is also common, a sign of camaraderie. In the United States, by contrast, some consider such touching invasive.

Russian, like other Europeans, perceive distances differently than Americans do. When a Russian says that he or she lives near something, an American imagines a 5–10 minute walk. In reality, a 20–30 minute trek may be in order.

# 46. POLITICS AND PARTIES

The 1917 Bolshevik Revolution brought the Communist Party to preeminence. Up until 1991 it was the only legal political party in the Soviet Union. Membership in the Communist Party was considered an honor and a privilege. Those desiring to join the Communist Party generally became members of the Young Komsomol (see Point 39, "Milestones"). They were expected to lead a life of commitment to party goals and service to society. Recommendations for membership and support from three current Communist Party members were required. Communist Party membership varied from 5–10% of the population.

Being a member of the Communist Part was a great help in one's career. Managers of factories, principals of high schools, and chairs of university departments, as well as people in higher positions, were all expected to be Party members. However, since the

Communist Party was a party of the proletariat, care was always taken to assure that a significant portion of the members were workers.

Since there was only one party in the Soviet Union, elections consisted not of two people competing against each other, but of the population voting for *one name* on the ballot. That person had been nominated by the Communist Party committee and then presented as a candidate by trade unions and workers' organizations. Usually, members of these organizations had already earlier approved the nomination.

On the day of voting, the whole population was expected to participate in the elections. Volunteers checked to see who had not voted toward closing time and made rounds encouraging and cajoling the public to vote. Indeed, while the Communist Party was in power, at least according to official statistics, over 99% of the population voted.

Prior to Mikhail Gorbachev's time, the government and the Communist Party functioned as one. Gorbachev's perestroika in the mid-1980s brought to life a number of political organizations and movements (such as the Democratic Platform), which—although they did not dare to call themselves parties—created the foundation for the multiparty system that now exists in Russia. The first political alternative movements opposed the ruling Communist Party on two major issues: totalitarian Stalinist ideology and proletarian internationalism, as exemplified in the slogan "Proletarians of the World Unite!" By the end of the 1980s Russia's major cities had "Popular Fronts" which integrated unofficial, pro-democratic, public groups and national–patriotic unions. Towards the end of the 1980s, Pamyat, a group within the All-Russian Society for the Preservation of Historical and Cultural Monuments, attracted public attention because of its anti-Semitic, nationalist orientation. After Chernobyl, ecologically and environmentally-minded groups, known as Greens, began to campaign on issues such as pollution and the presence of nuclear power stations in municipal areas. Another group, Memorial, strove to rehabilitate the victims of Stalinism and to raise funds for a memorial in their honor.

It was in 1989 that the first contested elections in the Soviet Union in over 70 years took place. Gorbachev decided that the seats for the Congress of People's Deputies of the Soviet Union should have competing candidates. For the first time, ordinary citizens became politically involved. In the process, many challenged the Communist Party officials. The physicist Andrei Sakharov was one of the deputies elected; he played a significant role when the Congress convened in May 1989. A political transformation took place as factions mushroomed.

At the Twenty-Eighth Communist Party Congress in July 1990, Gorbachev tried to maneuver between the right and left factions and satisfied neither. Toward the end of the Congress, Boris Yeltsin publicly announced his resignation from the Communist Party. This action was repeated the following day by St. Petersburg's (then Leningrad's) Mayor Anatoly Sobchak and Moscow's Mayor Gavril Popov. Other important leaders soon followed suit.

The failed coup of August 1991 against Gorbachev by the hard-liners signaled the end of the Communist Party as it had existed for over 75 years. The party split up into opposing factions which became separate parties. In December 1991 the Soviet Union was officially dissolved. Power passed to Boris Yeltsin. In June 1991 he was the first person to run in nationwide elections for President of Russia. He won with 60% of the popular vote. The dramatic events of September-October 1993, when Yeltsin's forces overwhelmed his opponents at the Communist-dominated Parliament, led to a proliferation of political parties.

In 1994 there were over 60 political parties registered with the Ministry of Justice in Russia. Parties are constantly changing: they mature, merge, split, or dissolve. Having no previous experience with a multiparty system, Russia is just learning how to deal with them. At this point, the parties are small and weak, and their allegiance is centered on a political leader more than a philosophy.

The parties can be divided into three groups and various subgroups. The three main groups may be called "democrats," "communists," and "nationalists."

There are about 30 democratically oriented parties. The more radical of them espouse a free market economy and a pro-Western foreign policy. Moderates, or social democrats (such as Yabloko and PRUA), advocate Western socialism and an independent foreign policy. The Centrists (for example, the Civic Union and the Democratic Party) gravitate toward the Chinese model and the Labor Party of England.

The Communist-oriented parties, of which there are about ten, want to see Russia become a superpower with a state-run, planned economy, following Marxist principles. The more conservative element of these parties denounces the Bolshevik heritage. They invoke "socialism with a human face" and an economy that is largely state-dominated but with some small allowance for private enterprise.

Nationalist parties share a common view of Russia as a superpower, with Russians as the dominant ethnic group. Their economic platforms, however, differ. Some of them advocate political pluralism and a mixed market economy, while others want to bring back the monarchy, Orthodoxy, and a state-run economy. Nationalist parties are often backed by paramilitary structures led by former "black berets" and Afghan war veterans. In the Parliamentary elections of December 1993, the misnamed Liberal Democratic Party, with Vladimir Zhirinovsky at its head, received 23% of the vote. Zhirinovsky has proclaimed his desire to see Russia become a colonial power and to regain the former territories of the Russian tsarist empire, including Poland, Finland, the three Baltic States, and even Alaska.

The resurgence of the Communist and nationalist parties and the number of votes they received in the December 1993 Parliamentary elections came as a shocking surprise to many who had expected the reformist parties to win. This resurgence may have been a response to economic difficulties: as inflation skyrocketed, many Russians lost faith in the reformers who were pushing for a free market economy. National pride was also a factor, as the country lost its international clout and superpower status. The military, which no longer enjoyed its preeminent position, was forced to absorb units from Eastern Europe and the former republics into already crowded quarters, and became dissatisfied. The rural population from Russia's vast countryside, traditionally conservative, saw no reason to switch to the new reformist groups.

# 47. PRIVACY

Privacy does not have the importance in a Russian's life that it does for those living in the West. Indeed, the Russian language does not have a word for "privacy." (There is however, an adjective meaning "private.") This is understandable for a society in which the needs and wishes of the "collective" are paramount and in which the word "private" has a negative connotation. Sharing of space and touching are considered positive values, while living an isolated life formerly invited a visit from the authorities. If one has nothing to hide, one does not need privacy. The ruling philosophy is: Live an exposed, explicit life, or you will be exposed.

# 48. PUNCTUALITY

The Russian view of punctuality is different from ours. Punching a time clock is an unknown notion for Russians. In a country where for over 70 years job security was assured and firings were rare, punctuality was of no great importance. A similar attitude exists toward deadlines. The Bolshoi Theater could plan to stage a new production of a ballet on a particular date, but if the director felt that the troupe was not ready, the opening would be put off. In a market-driven economy the show must go on as scheduled, and there would be pressure to meet the scheduled opening date. Similarly, in many a workplace a project might be due the next day, but workers would continue chatting at length about personal matters or leave to do personal shopping. A deadline would not be a high priority for them. Other workplaces, however, do demand punctuality and workers must even work overtime to meet deadlines.

On a social level, if you are invited to dinner at 6:00, do not show up at 6:00 P.M. sharp; 6:10, or even 6:30, is quite appropriate.

Theater performances and trains do, however, start and leave on time.

# 49. RELIGION

Although recent developments may somewhat challenge the following statement, outwardly religion does not seem to play an important role in the Russia of the early 1990s. For over 75 years Russians were told that religion was the "opium of the people" by its leaders, who proclaimed Russia an atheistic state, following the tenets of Marxism-Leninism. For over 75 years the Russian Orthodox Church, home of Russia's predominant religion before the 1917 Bolshevik Revolution, was severely limited in its ability to spread its message. For over 75 years those who chose to practice a religion risked discrimination in admittance to institutions of higher learning and at their jobs.

Following the tradition acquired from the Byzantine Empire when Prince Vladimir chose the Orthodox religion as the state religion in A.D. 998, religion in Russia was closely tied to the state and was subservient to it. This was true in tsarist times, as well as during the years of Communist rule. With the advent of glasnost, articles appeared in the Russian press claiming that the church had been infiltrated by KGB agents.

In the 1990s, religion in Russia again began playing a more public role. The Russian Orthodox Church slowly became more visible: for the first time in many years Easter church services were televised, the press published articles on religious topics, and Bibles in the Russian language and other religious items became available in stores. Religious services took place in churches that the authorities had turned into museums—in Moscow's Kremlin cathedrals and St. Basil's Cathedral. St. Petersburg's Kazan Cathedral, which had become a Museum of the History of Religion and Atheism, was converted into a Museum of the History of West European Christianity and the Orthodox Church.

With the demise of the Soviet Union and the discrediting (for many) of the Communist Party's philosophy, many Russians sought new sources for moral and spiritual guidance. Numerous religions stepped into the vacuum and began proselytizing in Russia: they range from the Church of the Unification (the "Moonies"), to Hare Krishnas, to Jehovah's Witnesses. Billy Graham made numerous visits to Russia, addressing thousands in stadium settings. The Russian Orthodox Church attempted to stop this flood of missionaries in July 1993 when it lobbied to have Parliament pass a law limiting access of Protestant evangelical groups to Russia. Eventually the restrictions were lifted. Yergin and Gustafson cite a conversation with a Russian Orthodox bishop who claimed that the influx of evangelical missionaries into Russia was a plot by the CIA to destabilize Russia.[1]

At the beginning of the twentieth century, the breakdown of religions in the Russian Empire was: Russian Orthodox (71%), Catholic (9%), Mohammedan (9%), Protestant (5%), and Jewish (3%). At present official figures on the breakdown of religions in Russia are not available. According to *Soviet Union: a country study*, in 1989, 50 million Soviet citizens belonged to the Russian Orthodox Church, 5.5 million to the Catholic Church, while 5 million espoused various Protestant religions, primarily Baptist. Islam

---

[1]Yergin & Gustafson, *Russia 2010,* p. 64

claimed the second largest number of believers, between 45 and 50 million. The majority of these were Sunni. It is not known how many people practiced Judaism. Prior to the Bolshevik Revolution there were some 5,000 functioning synagogues. Most of these were closed by Stalin, and others were closed by Khrushchev. The practice of Judaism became practically impossible.

# 50. RESTAURANTS

Before 1993, restaurants were far less common in Russia than in the United States. Consequently, it was difficult to get into the restaurants that did exist. In the bigger cities many restaurants are located in the hotels that cater to foreign visitors. In hotels with several restaurants, the most impressive serve only those who can pay with foreign currency. Most restaurants in hotels for foreign visitors are geared to the tourist trade and cater largely to groups. An individual tourist may get short shrift here and may be refused service completely.

Another type of restaurant in large cities is one that offers regional or ethnic cuisine, such as the Uzbekistan, Aragvi, and Baku restaurants in Moscow that serve Uzbek, Georgian, and Azerbaidzhani regional food. These restaurants are some of the city's finest, and Russians treasure their memories of eating in them. In order to get regional food, you must go to these rare, hard-to-get-into, regional restaurants. In the United States, those who are accustomed to choosing from several cuisines in the restaurants of one city block or on one menu find it surprising that in a city such as Moscow the nonregional restaurants will serve only Russian food, not an assortment of dishes from the many former Soviet republics.

Outings to the best restaurants are rare for Russians and are reserved for very special occasions. Because such an outing is quite expensive, Russians make an evening of it. They order extensive appetizers, a main course, and dessert, accompanied by mineral water and wine, champagne, vodka, and/or cognac. They expect service to be slow, with time perhaps for dancing to the restaurant's (generally very loud) orchestra between courses.

Because of the shortage of excellent restaurants and Moscow's population of nine million, it takes an effort to get into such a restaurant. Showing up at the door is unlikely to get you in, although a pack or two of Marlboro's or some money for the doorman may help. Calling a few days ahead and claiming to be part of a "foreign delegation" may get you reservations. It is important to know the hours of restaurants; many are closed from around 4:30 or 5:00 P.M. to 6:00 P.M.

The middle of the 1980s saw the appearance of cooperative restaurants "koopera*tiv*niye resto*rany*"/**коопера́тивные рестора́ны.** Families, or a strictly regulated number of people, were allowed to renovate an unused space and to set up a restaurant. The food in these restaurants was more expensive than in the state-run restaurants. Their main attraction was the attentive service they provided.

What about "middle-class" restaurants, small cafés, fast food places, carry-outs? In the early 1990s, places where one could stop in the evening for a quick bite on the way home from work or on the way to the theater were still rare, although their numbers are increasing. In theaters ticket holders can purchase open-faced sandwiches of cold cuts, smoked fish, cheese, or caviar to tide them over. People who are willing to eat "on the go" buy meat-, potato-, or cabbage-filled pastries from street vendors. Vendors also sell ice cream, even in winter.

Those Russians fortunate to have a dining room at their place of work may eat their main meal there. Others eat at cafeteria-style eating places, e.g., "Sto*lo*vaya," "Die*ti*cheskaya sto*lo*vaya," "Za*ku*sochnaya," or " Ka*fe*" (**Столо́вая, Диети́ческая столо́вая, Заку́сочная,** or **Кафе́**). They offer a soup and two or three main dishes and are of acceptable quality, although some Americans might label them "greasy spoon" establishments. Some restaurants specialize primarily in one dish, such as "pel*mæ*ni"/**пельме́ни,** or Siberian meat dumplings.

In restaurants everything is à la carte, including bread and butter. Fresh vegetables and fruits are generally not available out-of-season.

Moscow does have its three (but more are promised) McDonald's and two Pizza Huts. McDonald's sells for rubles; Pizza Hut has separate eating areas for those paying with rubles and with dollars. The pizzas sold for dollars are the same price as those sold in the West.

# 51. THE RUSSIAN LANGUAGE

Russian is a Slavic language. The Russian alphabet, known as the Cyrillic alphabet, "ki*r*llitsa"/**кири́ллица,** was created in the ninth century by two Slavonic monks, St. Cyril and St. Methodius. They borrowed letters from the Church Slavonic, Glagolitic, Hebrew, and Greek alphabets. The resulting alphabet, after some revision through the ages, consists of thirty-three letters.[2]

| Cyrillic Letter | | Name | Approximate Pronunciation in English |
|---|---|---|---|
| А | а | а | car |
| Б | б | бэ | but |
| В | в | вэ | visa |
| Г | г | гэ | gallery |
| Д | д | дэ | doctor |
| Е | е | е | yet |
| Ё | ё | ё | yolk |
| Ж | ж | жэ | measure |

---

[2]Morris, George W. et al., *Russian Face to Face,* Level 1, Lincolnwood (Chicago): National Textbook Company and Moscow: Russky Yazyk Publishers, 1993, p. 13.

| Cyrillic Letter | | Name | Approximate Pronunciation in English |
|---|---|---|---|
| З | з | зэ | **vi**sa |
| И | и | и | vi**s**a |
| Й | й | й (и кра́ткое) ("short" и) | bo**y** |
| К | к | ка | **c**lass, **k**ind |
| Л | л | эл (эль) | **l**uck |
| М | м | эм | **m**other |
| Н | н | эн | co**n**tact, **n**ame |
| О | о | о | **o**ld, n**o**te |
| П | п | пэ | **p**ull |
| Р | р | эр | **r**od |
| С | с | эс | **s**it |
| Т | т | тэ | **t**alk |
| У | у | у | f**oo**d |
| Ф | ф | эф | **ph**iloso**ph**er |
| Х | х | ха | **wh**o |
| Ц | ц | цэ | mee**ts** |
| Ч | ч | чэ | **ch**air, mat**ch** |
| Ш | ш | ша | **sh**op |
| Щ | щ | ща | **sh**eep |
| Ъ | ъ | твёрдый знак | hard sign [silent letter] |
| Ы | ы | ы | ch**a**rity |
| Ь | ь | мя́гкий знак | soft sign [silent letter] |
| Э | э | э | **e**xcuse |
| Ю | ю | ю | **u**se |
| Я | я | я | **y**ard |

Of these 33 letters, 10 are vowels (5 hard—**а, э, ы, о, у,** 5 soft—**я, е, и, ё, ю**), 21 are consonants, and 2 are voiceless signs (that signal the softness or hardness of the preceding consonant). Of the consonants, 5 letters have the same sound in both Russian and

English (б, к, м, т, з), while 5 letters are sometimes referred to as "false friends" because although they look exactly like Latin letters, they have a different sound in Russian (н, р, х, с, в). An additional 6 consonants look different from their English equivalents (д, ф, г, л, п, й). And finally, there are 5 consonants that have no English equivalents (ч, ш, щ, ц, ж).

Letters can represent one sound or two. The letter й placed after a vowel forms a diphthong. Words with more than one syllable have a stress, which may vary in a noun as it is declined (Russian has six cases) or a verb, when conjugated (Russian has six persons in the present tense). The presence or absence of stress on vowels influences the pronunciation of the vowels. However, Russian is a much more phonetic language than English—by and large it is pronounced the way it is written.

Russian is a language blessed with an extensive vocabulary. Translators and interpreters can attest to this fact: it takes about 10% more space and time to translate from English into Russian than from Russian into English.

Russian is spoken by the 150,000,000 people who make up the population of Russia and by the additional 143,000,000 people of the other former republics of the Soviet Union (1992 statistics). Despite the breakup of the Soviet Union, Russian remains the *lingua franca* of the former Soviet republics and of the countries of Eastern Europe. When East Europeans meet, a Hungarian and a Pole are more likely to know Russian than each other's language. Russian is even spoken in areas of Alaska, testimony to the fact that Russia at one time owned this territory.

If you are traveling to Russia, do try to master the Cyrillic alphabet. Signs at airports and train stations, streets, metro stations, and store names will be more comprehensible to you. If you can learn more—vocabulary, useful phrases for various situations, and how the grammar works—so much the better. Friendship and business deals will be easier to achieve. Russians greet attempts at the use of their language with appreciation. So if you are heading for Russia, pick up a Russian textbook, preferably accompanied by a tape, and start practicing.

A word of caution, however, about using Russian in the former republics of the Soviet Union. When addressing a Lithuanian, or an Uzbek, it might be wise first to apologize that you do not speak his or her language, and then to continue.

The Russian language played a significant role throughout the Soviet Union in eliminating illiteracy, which was at a level of 70% in the Russian empire at the time of the Bolshevik Revolution. Through universal education for the entire population, everyone was taught to read and write. In the case of non-Russians, these skills could then be transferred to their native languages.

# 52. RUSSIAN NATIONALITY AND CITIZENSHIP

A Russian internal passport, issued at age 16, indicates the following facts about a citizen of Russia: name, last name, patronymic, date of birth, place of birth, and nationality. In Russia, nationality is determined by biological origin. When both parents of a citizen are of the same nationality, i.e., Russian or Georgian, that nationality is indicated on the passport. However, if the parents have different nationalities, such as Russian and Jewish, at age 16 the person may choose which nationality will go into his or her passport. When both parents are Jewish, "Jewish" goes into the passport. Russians consider "Jewish" to be a nationality. The Russian language has two terms: "ev*rey*"/**еврéй**, to refer to a Jewish male, and "iu*dey*"/**иудéй**, to indicate a male who is a follower of the Jewish religion. In earlier periods of anti-Semitism, it was easy to identify who was of Jewish origin and to discriminate against them—not to admit them to universities, not to hire them for certain jobs, not to give them promotions. Russians who make a point of indicating a person's Jewishness frequently come across as being anti-Semitic.

Prior to its breakup, over 100 nationalities comprised the Soviet

Union. Each had its own language, history, religion, culture, national consciousness, and identity. The government strove to foster harmonious relations among the nationalities. By the late 1980s and into the 1990s, frictions—in some cases leading to wars—have come out in the open between a number of the nationalities. The Caucasus region has been especially volatile. A statement made by Dmitri Likhachov, an esteemed Russian academician, illuminates the uneasy relations between the many nationalities of Russia even today: "For me, patriotism is the love of one's country, while nationalism is the hatred of other peoples."[3]

## 53. THE RUSSIAN SOUL

In 1866 the poet Fyodor Tyutchev wrote:[4]

| | | |
|---|---|---|
| U *mom* Ro*ssiy*u ne pon*yat*, | Russia cannot be understood with the mind, | Умóм Россíю не понять, |
| Ar*shi*nom ob*shchim ne iz*merit; | Or measured with a common yardstick; | Аршíном óбщим не измéрить; |
| U ney o*so*bennaya stat— | She has a unique stature— | У ней осóбенная стать— |
| V Ro*ssiy*u *mozh*no *tol*ko *vy*erit. | One must simply believe in Russia. | В Россíю мóжно тóлько вéрить. |

Whenever a writer cannot explain something about Russians, the writer invariably comments on the mysteriousness of the Russian soul. What is the Russian soul? When did an interest in it appear? To some extent this was the result of the unusual interest in Russia in the middle of the nineteenth century when the works of Russian writers such as Ivan Turgenev (author of *Fathers and Sons*)

---

[3]Hedrick Smith, *The New Russians*, p. 393.
[4]K. Dogdanova, *Ten Russian Poets*, p. 242.

appeared in Europe. Who or what was Russia? Whatever could not be explained was answered by "Ah, it is the Russian soul!"

When a foreigner immersed in Russian culture thinks of the Russian soul, contradictions come to mind. Illustrative is the character Dmitri Karamazov in Fyodor Dostoevsky's *The Brothers Karamazov*. Literary critics sum up his character as generous, depraved, honest, deceitful, and dramatic. The Russian writer Dmitri Likhachov in his book *Zametki o russkom, Notes about Russianness* (*Заметки о русском*) mentions the Russian love for wide open spaces. He attributes this to the location in Russia of the largest plain in the world. Russians wandered across this vast plain, navigated the big rivers that were part of the plain, and gazed upon the never-ending skies. Russian painters such as Isaak Levitan in his work *Vladimirka* capture this Russian expanse. Russian towns frequently were situated on a high bank of a river, from which the inhabitants could gaze into the distance and into the waters and see the town's reflection and constant motion. When the heavy hand of authority was found to be too oppressive, Russians could choose to lose themselves in the vastness of the plain—going into the forests or setting off for distant Siberia. In such vastness, people become dependent on each other.

Russian generosity and kindness, especially to those in need of aid, is well-known. Foreign visitors, including the American author of this work, are the frequent beneficiaries of this kindness. An inquiry as to where something is located may well result in a Russian personally accompanying the visitor to the desired location. The use of affectionate diminutives is a linguistic expression of Russian kindness.

And while Likhachov acknowledges that many do indeed view Dmitri Karamazov as the embodiment of "Russianness," Likhachov considers early nineteenth-century writer Aleksander Pushkin as the essence of the Russian soul. Indeed, Dostoevsky himself named Pushkin as the ideal Russian.

# 54. THE SEASONS

In the United States summer begins with the summer solstice on June 21 or 22, autumn with the autuminal equinox on September 22 or 23, winter with the winter solstice on December 21 or 22, and spring with the vernal equinox about March 21. In Russia the seasons begin on the first of the months indicated above. Hence, summer starts June 1st, autumn, September 1st, and so forth. The northerly nature of Russia is fully appreciated if one spends August in Moscow. While many cities of the United States are sweltering in the "summer doldrums," Muscovites see the weather turn decidedly fall-like and start to wear fall clothing. In winter, twilight begins around 4:00 in the afternoon.

The northern orientation of Russia's geography contributes to its spectacular "White Nights." During June in St. Petersburg a newspaper can be read without any artificial light as late as midnight, while in Moscow it is still relatively light as late as 10:00 p.m.

# 55. SHOPPING

Prior to perestroika the shopping situation in Russia was predictable, though cumbersome. Instead of supermarkets with their multiple offerings, Russians shopped in separate stores for meat and poultry, milk products, bread, fruits and vegetables, and canned food products. All these stores were owned by the government; they were identified by the store names "Meat," "Bakery," and "Fruits and Vegetables." Prices were the same in all the stores, and there was no bargaining.

With the advent of cooperatives in the late 1980s a two-tiered system developed: there were government stores that sold sausage (when it was available) at prices to which the people were accustomed, and there were cooperative stores that sold higher quality sausage (which was almost always available) at higher prices. Foreign visitors could shop in special stores (Russian government-owned Beriozkas or joint-venture stores such as Moscow's "Sadko," where only hard currency was accepted (dollars, West German marks, French francs, etc.). Russians could not legally own hard currency and could not shop in these stores. Everyone could shop at the *"rynki"*/**рынки**, or markets, where Russians and people from the former Soviet republics sold produce (vegetables, fruits, and honey) from their private plots. In addition, cooperatives and government stalls sold meat when available. Bargaining was possible at the markets. Many Russian institutions offered their employees the privilege of special orders, or *"zakazy"*/**зака́зы**, enabling them to obtain products not normally available to the general public.

In the early 1990s, this system completely changed. Although there is still disagreement about whether Russians can legally own hard currency, they do in fact have it, and no stores are now closed to them. To supply the population with goods, new capitalists emerged who bought merchandise, frequently from abroad, and sold it from booths located near metro stations. Individuals desiring to earn an extra ruble (or dollar) are also in evidence at metro stations or other places where there is heavy foot traffic. Sellers buy items at government stores, add a percentage, and resell. Foreign and Russian clothing, liquor, Estée Lauder perfume, a carton of Russian milk, Heineken beer, canned food, a loaf of bread, Russian and American cigarettes, and unrefrigerated meat can all be bought in this manner. Prices vary considerably. Periodically the Russian media warns the public about goods purchased at such stalls. Perishable items (such as a jar of caviar or milk) may be spoiled, or liquor may have been tampered with. Foreign visitors are well advised to avoid this mode of commerce unless accompanied by Russians whom they trust and who know which vendors are reliable.

The vast majority of stores are still stores owned by the government. At such stores, the buyer chooses certain items (such as a loaf of rye bread, six bagels, and 300 grams of candy), finds out the cost of these items from a salesperson, goes to a cashier to pay for the goods, then returns to the salesperson with a receipt to pick up the purchases. Russian cashiers do not put change into the buyer's hand; instead, it is placed on the counter.

Many Russian stores, banks, cleaning establishments, drugstores, and service stores, close for an hour for lunch, generally between one and three o'clock. In addition, stores, even airport stores that cater to tourists and earn greatly desired foreign currency, may be closed for an "inventory" or a "cleaning day." It behooves the tourist not to leave important purchases until the last day.

# 56. SHORTAGES AND DEFICIENCIES

The end of the 1980s and the early 1990s were years of shortages, or "defi*tsit*"/**дефици́т**, when food, clothing, and household items disappeared from the stores. One month it could be soap—or toilet paper, toothpaste, coffee, tea, underwear, socks, matches, caviar, wine, cooking utensils, toilet seats, paint, or wallpaper. Uncertain of what items would or would not be available, Russian shoppers bought up everything in sight to hoard goods against the day these items became unavailable.

# 57. SLOGANS AND STATUES

On top of some Russian buildings there are slogans such as "Long Live Communism," "Our Party is the Brains, Conscience, and Honor of Our Century," "Communism = Soviet Power and the

Electrification of the Entire Country," and "Lenin Lived, Lenin Lives, Lenin Will Live." Prior to perestroika such slogans were ubiquitous, appearing on outside billboards, the tops of buildings, as backgrounds behind podiums inside buildings, and on bulletin boards. Portraits of Lenin and other heroes of the 1917 Revolution were obligatory in every city and village office; statues of these heroes were in the squares of Russian towns and cities.

Since 1991 the majority of these slogans and statues have been removed, though Lenin can still be seen, especially in areas of the country where conservative leaders are in power. A similar phenomenon occurred with Stalin. Prior to 1956, pictures and statues of Stalin were to be seen everywhere. After Khruschchev delivered his "de-Stalinization speech," Stalin's body was taken out of the government mausoleum in Moscow and his portraits and statues disappeared.

# 58. SPORTS

The most popular sports in Russia are soccer and hockey. Starting with grade school, Russian youngsters are encouraged to participate in sports. An eighth grade student in a Moscow school will do some gymnastic exercises in the fall, go cross-country skiing twice a week during the winter season, and in the spring practice *lyog*kaya at*le*tika," track and field (**лёгкая атлётика**). The gyms of high schools and institutions of higher learning are popular places for students to congregate and for organized groups of youngsters to compete. "Pick-up" squads, randomly gathering, are not a common practice. The American system of after-school intramural sports, or sports competition among schools or universities within a city, is absent in Russia.

Students with an interest in sports attend special sports schools. Prior to the 1990s these schools were supported financially by the

Soviet government. Coaches were on the lookout for promising athletes. The ultimate payoff for both the coach and the athlete was a gold medal in the Olympics. In the heyday of Soviet sports, many such medals were earned in gymnastics, track and field, weightlifting, basketball, and ice hockey. Sports were used as a measuring stick for the superiority of communism over capitalism. Top athletes received significant perks from the Soviet government—splendid apartments, cars, permission to travel abroad, and cushy jobs. With the breakup of the Soviet Union, many of the athletes from the republics have chosen to compete under the flags of their own countries. In addition, the government no longer allots the money to sports that it once did.

Traditionally, large factories have also encouraged sports among the workers. During nonworking hours, workers can choose to participate in factory-sponsored teams. The most popular sports for workers are soccer and volleyball. Chess, considered a sport, also has its admirers and clubs. If a factory is large, a number of teams may compete with each other, or one factory may compete with another.

Even though the money allotted to train athletes for major competitions has decreased, emphasis on sports remains strong nevertheless. The maxim "a healthy mind in a healthy body" continues to be popular in Russia.

The disintegration of the former Soviet Union resulted in the disintegration of the teams sent to Olympic competition. The 1992 Olympics saw the countries of the Baltics competing as separate nations; the majority of the other former Soviet Republics competed for the last time as the "Unified team." However, if a sportswoman from Ukraine won, the Ukrainian flag, not the Soviet Union flag, was raised. At the 1994 Olympics in Lillehammer, Norway, the former Soviet republics competed under their own flags.

For the ordinary Russian the concept of "sports" also encompasses nature activities—not just the very popular cross-country skiing, but also gathering mushrooms (see Point 41, "Mushrooms") and berries.

# 59. STARING

Staring is not considered as impolite in Russia as it is in the United States. Foreign visitors, especially before the 1990s, were stared at in Russia. Since the 1990s, as Western goods have become more available, the distinction between Russians and foreign visitors is less evident. Nevertheless, especially outside the more heavily populated cities of Russia and the former Soviet Union, foreign visitors may still find themselves objects of curiosity. No offense is meant however.

Prior to the 1990s, staring at foreign visitors at times led to an offer to purchase what was being worn or carried. With Western goods more available lately, there has been a decrease in such solicitations. A Russian or a foreign visitor who becomes the object of unwelcome staring can say "Che*vo* vy na me*nya* smo*tr*ite?", Why are you staring at me? (**Чего вы на меня смотрите?**)

# 60. STREET NAMES AND ADDRESSES

If you are invited to visit a Russian apartment, you should be aware of the following, specific to the Russian situation. Russian street addresses tend to be much smaller than in the United States. Buildings are numbered in sequence (even numbers on one side, odd numbers on the other) from the beginning of a street, and this sequence does not depend on "blocks," a concept which is almost nonexistent in Russia (see below). As a result, street numbers are lower in Russia than in the United States; it is unusual to have a four- or five-digit building number.

Apartment numbers, on the other hand, are frequently very large. Since some buildings consist of hundreds, sometimes even a thousand apartments, it is possible to have an address such as "Pro*spekt Mi*ra" / **Проспект Мира**, "dom 317"/дом 317, "*ko*rpus 4"/

ко́рпус 4, "kvar*tira* 5227"/**кварти́ра** 5227. If you are given such an address, with "Pro*spekt Mi*ra"/ **Проспе́кт Ми́ра** as the street, "dom 317"/**дом** 317 as the equivalent of the idea of a *block,* "*kor*pus 4"/ **ко́рпус** 4 as the specific building within the block, "kvar*tira* 5227"/ **кварти́ра** 5227 as the apartment number, and you intend to visit, it is wise to ask two questions: what floor, "e*tazh,*"/**эта́ж**, and what entrance, "pod*yezd*"/**подъе́зд**, you should use. Otherwise, you may spend a long time searching for the right part of the building and the right floor.

When a house is located at the crossing of two streets, the address indicates this fact. Thus, "*Plot*nikov pere*ulok, Dom 2/8"/ **Пло́тников пере́улок, Дом 2/8**, means that the house is number 2 on Plotnikov Street, but number 8 on the street which it crosses. The name of this secondary street is not given in an address.

(See Point 37, "Letters, Greeting Cards, and Announcements," on how to address correspondence to Russians.)

# 61. THE "STRONG MAN" CONCEPT

The concept of the "strong man"—"*tvyor*dy chelo*vyek*"/"*kryep*ky khoz*yain,*" "*sil*naya *lich*nost" (**тве́рдый челове́к/кре́пкий хозя́ин, си́льная ли́чность**)—is well known in Russian culture. The attitude toward Ivan the Terrible, Stalin, and other leaders in Russian history is tied to the Russian attitude toward the strong man, whoever he may be. The idea started with fairy tales and how they presented the image of the tsar. Peasants, often abused by overbearing, inconsiderate landlords, believed that landlords could abuse them only because the tsar did not know about their actions. "If only he knew about it, he would do something." After the Bolshevik Revolution, during the period of Stalin's excesses, his victims went to their deaths believing that Stalin's enemies, not Stalin, were responsible for their unjust treatment. The West values individualism and freedom and mistrusts authority. Russians value order and security and believe that firmness from their leaders is essential.

# 62. SUPERSTITIONS

There are a number of superstitions that influence the behavior of Russians. Prior to leaving for a trip, they sit down in silence for a few minutes. Failure to do so it is believed will result in some calamity, conveyed by the expression "ne *bu*det do*ro*gi"/**не бу́дет доро́ги** (you will have no road). Once one leaves the house, it is considered bad luck to return for any reason. Should one be forced to return, however, danger can be averted by looking in the mirror before one leaves the house the second time.

It is important for Russians not to appear to be joyous about something ahead of time, lest the evil eye fall on one. They knock on wood three times, or spit over the left shoulder, or say "*chto*by ne *sglaz*it," so that no one will curse you (**что́бы не сгла́зить**). Birthday wishes or wedding anniversary congratulations are not conveyed ahead of the actual day of celebration. Expectant mothers do not purchase anything for their babies until they are born lest the evil eye harm the baby. After a baby is born, some parents choose not to show the baby to anyone for two or three weeks so that no one can harm it by complimenting it.

Russians do not sit at the corner of a table or shake hands over a threshold. Salt spilled on the table means there will be a fight in the family. A broken mirror portends some kind of misfortune. If a bird flies into a room, there will be a death in one's closest circle. If a cat, especially a black one, crosses the street, Russians believe that to avoid misfortune they should change the direction in which they are going, or wait until someone else walks in front of them. A spider crawling up a wall forecasts good news, while one crawling down, bad news. A Russian whose left palm itches expects to receive some money. If the left nostril itches, however, some imbibing will soon take place. If a knife falls, a male visitor can be expected, while if it is either a spoon or a fork—a female visitor.

If two friends accidentally knock heads, they should immediately knock heads again, otherwise there will be an argument between them. Likewise if a person steps on someone's foot, that person should step on the foot of the person who originally misstepped or an argument will take place between them. Russians who give medicine or a sharp object as a gift to someone are given some token money for the item.

# 63. TEA

Tea has been the most popular nonalcoholic drink in Russia ever since it arrived from Mongolia in the seventeenth century. Tea is taken with breakfast, after the midday meal (dinner for Russians), at mid-afternoon break, and after supper. (Tea with a meal is highly unusual; no amount of pleading at Intourist restaurants, for example, would produce tea until dessert is served.) Except for the Krasnodar region, Russia does not produce its own tea. Prior to the breakup of the Soviet Union, tea from the Georgian Republic was sold. Its green tea was considered medicinal. The most popular tea is imported from India and Sri Lanka. Of English and American teas, Earl Grey is a special favorite of Russians. These days any good tea is an appreciated gift.

While the preparation of tea is not as important in Russia as it is in Japan, certain traditions are nevertheless preserved. Loose tea is placed in a scalded teapot, hot water is poured over it, and a tea cozy placed over the teapot. After the tea has steeped for a few minutes, a little of the strong mixture is poured into teacups or a glass in a metal holder called a "podsta*ka*nnik"/**подстака́нник**, and boiling water is added to taste. Individual tea bags are rare in Russia and are not considered real tea.

The traditional way of serving tea is through the use of a samovar or "self-boiler." Water is poured into the samovar, an urn-like metal container. Electric samovars appeared in the twentieth century. The traditional ones, however, contain a cylindrical tube into which hot coals are placed to heat the water. A strong tea mixture, "za*va*rka"/**заварка**, is prepared in a small teapot. Tea is served by pouring a bit of the "za*va*rka" into a glass, then adding water from the samovar. When not in use, the teapot is placed on top of the samovar and a tea cozy placed on top of it.

# 64. THE TELEPHONE

The first telephone was installed in Russia in 1896. At times foreign callers and visitors may feel that telephone technology has not advanced much beyond that date. In the 1990s one-third of all phone calls made reach the wrong party. A frequently heard expression is "Vy ne tu*da* po*pa*li," You didn't land where you expected, i.e., you reached the wrong party (**Вы не туда попали**). Upon reaching the desired party, the phone conversation may still be unsatisfactory, due to static on the line. Phone conversations are frequently cut off. Hence the unnerving tendency of Russians to say "al*lo*, al*lo*"/**алло, алло,** to verify that a connection still exists at the slightest pause in a conversation. Nevertheless, those who have telephones are grateful. (According to official Soviet data, in 1986 only 28% of urban and 9.2% of rural families had telephones.) Not infrequently in businesses, dormitories, and communal housing there exist communal telephones that are shared over a number of floors. In such cases one needs to call a number of times until the right party picks up the telephone.

For people living in Russian villages or spending a few days at their dachas, communication with the outside is possible from post offices which have one or two phone booths with long distance connections. A Russian who wants to make a phone call fills out a form indicating the place to be called, the desired phone number, and the number of minutes he or she wishes to speak. Having paid in advance for the conversation, he or she waits until called to go to the booth. If the party called is not available, or if the phone conversation takes less time than expected, a refund is in order.

Phone conversations tend to be brief in Russia. The frequently poor quality of phone connections plays a role. So does the desire to exchange information face to face, not via telephone. Fear that the telephone may still be bugged in the 1990s and the certainty that it has been bugged in the past keep Russians from revealing anything of importance on the telephone.

Travelers who arrive in Russia without the home phone numbers of those they want to get in touch with may find it difficult to obtain them. Residential telephone books do not exist. (A former resident of Kiev, however, asserts that he had one.) To get a phone number, you need to go to a "Spravochnoe byuro," Information Bureau (Спра́вочное бюро́), give the person's name and year of birth, pay a small fee, and return later (a few hours later) for the information. "Yellow Pages" telephone books have been available in limited editions in the largest cities since the 1960s; and in the 1970s the telephone company instituted an "Information" number, 09, by which operators give out desired phone numbers. In 1993 a fee of 125 rubles was charged for non-government business phone number information. The 1990s have also seen numerous business phone books published by foreign companies.

Russians answer the telephone with one of these three statements: "Da?"/"Allo"/"Slushayu vas," Yes?/Hello/I am listening to you (Да?/Алло́/Слу́шаю вас). Conversations, as mentioned above, tend to be brief. When calling a store to find out its hours, for example, it behooves one to listen carefully, because having given an answer, the person will immediately hang up, not giving the caller a chance to verify the information. Answering machines are extremely rare in Russia. Offices cannot transfer a phone call from one telephone to another or set up conference calls.

People who expect to do business in and from Russia have a number of possible communication channels. There are business offices (such as one located in the GUM store on Red Square) that offer services such as faxing outside Russia, receiving faxes, and photocopying. While waiting for these services to be performed, a (foreign-currency) bar is at your disposal. Electronic mail can be set up in an office or an apartment. For this you need a telephone, a computer, a 2,400 baud, error-correcting modem, plus the appropriate software and a contract with an electronic-mail company. Foreign businesses or individuals seeking to obtain a direct telephone line in the early 1990s had to pay $20,000.

One may contact operators from the United States by dialing an access number and giving the American operator a credit card number. Such calls are fast, efficient—and expensive. In 1993 the first minute cost $7.00, with a $3.00 charge for each additional minute. In theory it is possible to direct dial Europe, the United States, etc., from certain areas of Russia, such as Moscow. However, experience has proven that the United States line is constantly busy. Less busy is the telephone number to "order" more expensive operator-assisted international or long-distance phone calls.

When Russians give a telephone number, they say the first three digits as a unit, followed by the next two as a unit, and again the last two as a unit. Thus 435–34–98 would be "four hundred thirty five/ thirty four/ninety eight."

# 65. TEMPERATURE

Temperature in Russia is measured in degrees of Celsius (Centigrade). To convert to the Fahrenheit scale, multiply the Celsius temperature by $\frac{9}{5}$, and then add 32.

Russia is a vast country with eleven time zones. The entire country is farther north than Los Angeles. Both St. Petersburg and Moscow lie to the north of Quebec, Canada. Average high (Fahrenheit) temperatures in three Russian cities are:

|  | **Moscow** | **St. Petersburg** | **Irkutsk** (Siberia) |
|---|---|---|---|
| January | 14 | 23 | 9 |
| February | 19 | 24 | 7 |
| March | 29 | 33 | 21 |
| April | 43 | 45 | 36 |
| May | 60 | 58 | 52 |
| June | 67 | 66 | 67 |
| July | 71 | 71 | 70 |
| August | 68 | 66 | 66 |
| September | 56 | 57 | 52 |
| October | 44 | 45 | 38 |
| November | 28 | 34 | 4 |
| December | 17 | 26 | 3 |

The northern orientation of Moscow should not be taken as an indication that long underwear is in order when planning a visit. Russians like to have their apartments, houses, places of work, metro stations, etc., considerably warmer than Americans. Inside buildings long underwear may make one uncomfortably warm. From October to early April what is essential is that one have a warm long coat, hat, scarf, gloves, and high, sturdy, waterproof boots.

# 66. TIME OF DAY

In Russia the 24-hour system is used to give the official time for travel timetables, as well as for television schedules, theater performances, film showings, and sports events.

The 24-hour system is also frequently used in everyday conversations. A 4:00 P.M. social get-together or a business appointment is at "16 hours" for a Russian. (If the time mentioned is after 12 noon, just subtract 12 from the quoted time to determine the hour.)

When the 24-hour system is not used, Russian, which does not use A.M. and P.M., follows the clock time with the genitive case of *morning, day, evening,* and *night:* "ut*ra* (**утра́**), "dnya" (**дня**), "*vy*echera" (**ве́чера**), and "*no*chi" (**но́чи**). Although the Russian system of telling time is rather complicated, with different grammar rules for time up to the half hour and after it, the popularity of digital watches and clocks has made it acceptable to say che*ty*re *so*rok pyat, 45 minutes after 4 (**четы́ре со́рок пять**), as opposed to bez *ch*etverti pyat, "without" a quarter to five (**без че́тверти пять**).

When writing time, a period is placed between the hour and the minutes, instead of a colon: 4.16.

# 67. TOILETS

Foreign visitors should be aware that the condition of Russian public toilets can frequently be a source of consternation. In out-of-the-way places, even those frequently visited by tourists, toilets may be no more than a hole in the ground in a wooden shack. Even where modern plumbing exists, the toilets are frequently dirty. Toilet paper is extremely rare in public places, so it is always wise to carry tissues. The late 1980s saw an improvement in the conditions of those restrooms that were purchased by cooperatives, cleaned, repaired, and more carefully maintained. Many Russians consider it worth the rubles charged to use these clean facilities. Public restrooms continue to leave much to be desired.

# 68. *TY* AND *VY*, "YOU"—FAMILIAR AND FORMAL (ТЫ AND ВЫ)

Family members, close friends, children, and animals are addressed by the familiar "*ty*," you (ты). (Compare to the French **tu** and the Spanish **tú**.) Other people, and more than one person, are addressed by "*vy*," you (вы). The "*vy*"/вы form, together with the first name and patronymic, is the preferred form of address among Russians, even among colleagues who have worked together for many years. In some families, children address their parents with "*vy*"/вы. In correspondence, "*vy*"/вы is capitalized when addressing one person, but not when it is directed to two or more people.

Knowing when to switch from "*vy*"/вы to "*ty*"/ты takes considerable experience, and foreign visitors should use the "*vy*"/вы form when in doubt. Serfs and servants were historically addressed by the familiar form. The inappropriate use of "*ty*"/ты is a form of insult. To go from the "*vy*"/вы form to "*ty*"/ты, two people pour a drink, link arms, drink, then kiss each other once (or three times). This ceremony is referred to as "bruder*shaft*"/брудершáфт.

The use of "*ty*" or "*vy*" influences the endings of verbs: one says "*ty* chita*esh*," you [singular or familiar] are reading (ты читáешь), but "*vy* chita*ete*," you [plural or polite] are reading (вы читáете). Even the most common way of saying "hello" is affected. "*Zdravstvuy*"/Здрáвствуй is said to people with whom one is on a "*ty*" basis, but "*zdravstvuyte*"/здрáвствуйте to people with whom "*vy*" is used.

# 69. TRANSPORT, TRAFFIC, ACCIDENTS, AND HOW TO COPE WITH A MILITIAMAN (POLICEMAN)

The major Russian cities, which until the late 1980s were relatively free of traffic jams, have begun to experience road congestion. The rush hours, "cha*sy* pik"/**часы́ пик,** are from 7:00 to 9:00 in the morning, and 4:00 to 7:00 in the evening. During this time, metro cars, buses, trolleys, and the streets of the cities are very crowded. Weekends bring no relief, because a large part of the population heads for dachas in the countryside.

Russia has been justifiably proud of its transportation system, with the metro systems in Moscow and St. Petersburg, and with bus, trolley, and streetcar networks in other cities. However, as more people move into cities and the number of vehicles is reduced to save energy, the transportation system has become overloaded. Russians complain that with fewer buses on the streets it is taking them longer and longer to get to work.

Visitors should be aware that many Russian drivers drive as if they, not the pedestrian, have the right of way on Russian streets. It is always wise to look in all directions before crossing a street. At many street intersections in big cities, underground passageways, "pere*kho*dy"/**перехо́ды,** have been constructed. Crossing the street without using them may lead to a "shtraf," fine (**штраф**).

An unusual feature of driving in Russian cities is the U-turn permitted, when indicated by the appropriate street sign, in the middle of a street.

Traffic accidents are a common sight in Russia. First of all, traffic laws are often ignored. Moreover, even though there are frequent checks by the militia, drunken drivers abound; and the result is many accidents. "*Sko*raya *po*moshch," the ambulance service (**Ско́рая по́мощь**), used to have, by and large, an excellent reputation. The ambulances arrived quickly and were staffed by skilled doctors. By early 1994, however, the quality of this service had declined. The ambulances, a "Rafik" brand van produced in

Latvia, were in need of repair, but parts were unavailable because Latvia required payment in hard currency.

There are two types of militia, as Russian policemen are called. "Militsio*ne*ry"/**милиционéры** are in charge of maintaining order on the streets and in public places where people gather; "Ga*ish*niki"/ **ГАИшники** are in charge of traffic. They see that road laws are obeyed, set up roadblocks to check on the sobriety and legality of drivers, stop motorists for speeding, and check on weight limits of trucks. When a traffic policeman stops a Russian driver, what happens next depends on the personalities involved. Many Russian drivers carry emergency gifts for the Gaishnik in order to favorably influence him. If a Gaishnik is interested in a "gift," he is likely to invite the offender to his car, so that the gift can be offered in private.

# 70. VACATIONS

The length of vacations varies. Most Russians generally have 24 working days (i.e., a month) of vacation per year. Clerical staff in schools, factories, etc., receive from 12 to 18 working days. Teachers, irrespective of where they work, receive 48 working days. People working in difficult or dangerous conditions, such as in Russia's far north, may receive additional vacation days. By agreeing to work overtime on weekends or holidays, Russians may increase the number of their vacation days. Prior to the late 1980s, an ideal vacation for a Russian was a "pu*tyov*ka"/**путёвка**, a "subsidized vacation package deal," which included room and board at a sanatorium. Unlike the English meaning, these sanatoriums are not medical establishments, although doctors and nurses may be on the premises. The scarcity of hotels and the poor roads make the "family driving vacation," so common in the Western world, risky in Russia. Students and other adventurous souls frequently travel and camp along the way.

After the late 1980s and into the 1990s, as republics seceded from the Soviet Union, Russians frequently were not welcome in many places that had been popular (e.g., the Black Sea and Baltic Sea resorts and the Caucasus), and the choices for vacation spots decreased. However, the vastness of Russia (the largest country in the world) offers the residents many choices. While many couples vacation together, it is not unusual for husbands and wives to take their vacations separately.

Foreign visitors traveling to Russia on business should be aware that frequently upon arriving in Russia they may be told that key personnel are on vacation, even if the visit has been planned for a number of months. While on vacation, even Russian professionals normally do not contact their place of work. This practice can be worse than annoying for foreign visitors in Russia on business.

# 71. VODKA AND DRINKING

Vodka, the most popular drink in Russia, is made from potatoes, wheat, or rye. In restaurants vodka (as well as other popular drinks such as cognac and wine) is sold by the gram—100 grams, 200 grams, etc. A small decanter is 500 grams. Vodka bottles sold for local consumption do not have a reclosable bottle top. This leads to many jokes about the fact that once a bottle has been opened, it needs to be emptied, frequently leading to a hangover. To get over the hangover, one needs to have a drink, but since the bottle cannot be closed, it again needs to be emptied, and the cycle recommences.

Through the centuries, Russians have been singled out for their heavy drinking. Almost all accounts of Russia comment on drunkenness, frequently of a "binge" nature. It has been suggested that the penchant for this type of drinking has its origins in the practice of wrapping Russian children in tight swaddling clothes, from which they were released on occasion for a wild romp. Drinking vodka, cognac, or moonshine to excess is called the "ze*lyo*ny zmey," green serpent (**зелёный змей**), while the practice of drinking constantly is referred to as "podda*vat*"/**поддавáть**. To gesture that someone is inebriated or wants to drink, Russians rub two fingers together under their chins, or by the side of one of their ears.

Do not expect to be served cocktails when visiting a Russian home. On the table there may be bottles of champagne, wine, vodka, or cognac. Vodka and cognac are drunk "neat" from a shot glass, immediately followed by a bit of pickle, rye bread, sausage, or herring. This practice is repeated again and again. Foreign visitors not used to such drinking need to be wary, lest they end up under the table. Pleading doctor's orders or religious convictions may be in order even if untrue.

Although a guest may successfully beg off from drinking, the offering of a toast is nearly obligatory. Russians highly value the ability to offer toasts. Generally the first toast is made by the host or hostess or an honored guest. It is not unusual for the toasts to continue unabated throughout the course of a meal.

# 72. WEIGHTS AND MEASURES

The metric system is used in Russia.

| | | |
|---|---|---|
| **миллиме́тр** | milli*metr* | millimeter (.0394 inch) |
| **сантиме́тр** | santi*metr* | centimeter (.3937 inch—less than half an inch) |
| **метр** | metr | meter (39.37 inches—about one yard and 3 inches) |
| **киломе́тр** | kilo*metr* | kilometer (.6214 of a mile—about $\frac{5}{8}$ of a mile) |
| **литр** | litr | liter (1.0567 quarts—a fraction over a liquid quart) |
| **грамм** | gramm | gram (.0353 ounce) |
| **килогра́мм** | kilo*gramm* | kilogram (35.27 ounces—about 2.2 pounds) |

**Conversion tables**

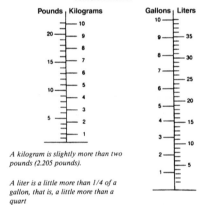

A kilogram is slightly more than two pounds (2.205 pounds).

A liter is a little more than 1/4 of a gallon, that is, a little more than a quart

A kilometer is approximately 5/8 of a mile.

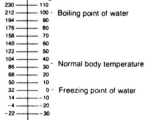

# 73. WORK AND PROFESSIONS

The Russian workday generally starts at 9:00 or 9:30 A.M., or frequently at 10:00 A.M. Factory workers, however, may start as early as 7:30 or 8:00 A.M. An hour-long lunch (frequently dinner, the main meal of the day) is taken around 1:00 P.M., and a tea break at 3:30 or 4:00. Work stops around 5:00 or 6:00 P.M. As in most cultures there is wide variety in the Russian work ethic. Many Russians are hardworking and conscientious and take great pride in the timeliness and quality of their work. Some remember the times during the Stalin years when showing up at work even a few minutes late resulted in being arrested. During the years of central economic planning, the end of an economic plan at the end of a month resulted in deadlines that had to be kept and plans to be fulfilled at all costs. Nevertheless, the many years of government policy of low salaries, employment for all of its citizens, and extremely rare firings has resulted in a lax work ethic. The saying, "The government pretends to pay us and we pretend to work," often still seems to be in effect.

The changes in Russian society since 1991 make it difficult to gauge public attitudes toward the most popular and/or respected professions in Russia. Prior to 1991 the most respected professions in Russia were party and trade-union bosses, diplomats, dentists, journalists, radio and television broadcasters, and lawyers (known as "advo*kat*y"/**адвока́ты**). Popular also were auto mechanics and all jobs having to do with hard currency or foreign trade companies. Catering to the intelligentsia (see Point 34, "The Intelligentsia") ensured that the professions of artists, writers, and scientists were valued and included perks, such as free vacations passes or "pu*tyov*ki"/**путёвки**. Since 1991, these professions have lost both their prestige and their perks. Increasingly important, though not necessarily respected, in contemporary Russia is the businessman, the entrepreneur, the owner of a cooperative or international venture. The generation of Russians who have grown up believing that making a profit is immoral resent the success of people engaged in such activities. "They do not create anything themselves, only charge us more for what someone else has already produced" is a common complaint by those critical of the new ways.

The fields of medicine and engineering, highly respected in the West, are somewhat less so in Russia. Except for highly specialized surgeons who are respected and receive relatively large salaries, doctors tend to be females and are paid no more than schoolteachers, another largely female, low-paying profession. For engineers, the situation is a bit more complicated. In order to qualify as an engineer, one needs to be a graduate of a technical engineering institute. Competition for admission to these institutes is strong, and the jobs the graduates received within the former Soviet Union were impressive. And yet when some of these graduates emigrated to the West, some of them were told that they were not "engineers" by Western standards.

The role of women is changing in Russia in the 1990s. During the Soviet period women were officially treated as equals with men. They were provided generous maternity leave, and their jobs were held for up to three years after childbirth. They worked in typically female positions—as doctors and teachers—as well as in jobs that demanded physical strength: construction work and house painting. They were managers of factories, stores, and research labs. Much was made of their presence in the government and party, though they rarely held top, policy-making positions. In the 1990s, with the drive for a market economy, proportionately more women than men, especially women with children, have been forced to join the unemployment ranks.

# SELECTED BIBLIOGRAPHY AND
# ADDITIONAL READINGS

Batalden, Stephen R. and Batalden, Sandra L. *The Newly Independent States of Eurasia: Handbook of Former Soviet Republics.* Phoenix: The Oryx Press, 1993.

Bogdanova, K., compiler and editor. *Ten Russian Poets.* Moscow: Progress Publishers, 1979.

Bogert, Carroll. "What's Right With Russia," *Newsweek.* June 21, 1993, p. 45.

Corten, Irina H. *Vocabulary of Soviet Society and Culture.* Durham, North Carolina: Duke University Press, 1992.

Edwards, Mike. "A Broken Empire," *National Geographic.* Volume 183, No. 3 (March 1993), pp. 4–53.

Gerhart, Genevra. *The Russian's World; Life and Language.* New York: Harcourt Brace Jovanovich, Inc., 1974.

Gunther, John. *Inside Russia Today.* New York: Harper & Brothers, 1958.

Hingley, Ronald. *Russian Writers and Society, 1825–1904.* New York: McGraw-Hill Book Company, 1967.

McDowell, Bart. *Journey Across Russia: The Soviet Union Today.* Washington, D.C.: National Geographic Society, 1977.

Morris, George W., Vyatyutnev, Mark N., and Vokhmina, Lilia L., *Russian Face to Face,* Level 1, Lincolnwood (Chicago): National Textbook Company and Moscow: Russky Yazyk Publishers, 1993.

Riasanovsky, Nicholas V. *A History of Russia,* fourth edition. New York: Oxford University Press, 1984.

Richmond, Yale. *From Nyet to Da; Understanding the Russians.* Yarmouth, Maine: Intercultural Press, 1992.

Smith, Hedrick. *The Russians.* New York: Ballatine Books, 1976.

Smith, Hedrick. *The New Russians.* New York: Random House, 1990.

Starr, S. Frederick. "The Waning of the Russian Intelligentsia," *Newsletter of the American Association for the Advancement of Slavic Studies.* Vol. 32, No. 2 (March, 1992), pp. 1–2.

Terras, Victor, ed. *A Handbook of Russian Literature.* New Haven: Yale University Press, 1985.

Utechin, S. V. *A Concise Encyclopedia of Russia.* New York: E. P. Dutton & Co., Inc., 1964.

Vishnevskaya, Galina. *Galina, A Russian Story.* Translated by Guy Daniels. New York: Harcourt Brace, 1985.

Yergin, Daniel and Thane Gustafson. *Russia 2010 and What It Means for the World.* New York: Random House, 1993.

Zickel, Raymond E., ed. *Soviet Union: a country study,* second edition. Federal Research Division, Library of Congress, 1991, Headquarters, Department of Army, DA Pan 550–95.

# INDEX

# INDEX

# FOREIGN LANGUAGE BOOKS

**Multilingual**
The Insult Dictionary:
  How to Give 'Em Hell in 5 Nasty
  Languages
The Lover's Dictionary:
  How to be Amorous in 5 Delectable
  Languages
Multilingual Phrase Book
Let's Drive Europe Phrasebook
CD-ROM "Languages of the World":
  Multilingual Dictionary Database

**Spanish**
Vox Spanish and English Dictionaries
NTC's Dictionary of Spanish False Cognates
Nice 'n Easy Spanish Grammar
Spanish Verbs and Essentials of Grammar
Getting Started in Spanish
Spanish à la Cartoon
Guide to Spanish Idioms
Guide to Correspondence in Spanish
The Hispanic Way

**French**
NTC's New College French and English
  Dictionary
French Verbs and Essentials of Grammar
Real French
Getting Started in French
Guide to French Idioms
Guide to Correspondence in French
French à la Cartoon
Nice 'n Easy French Grammar
NTC's Dictionary of *Faux Amis*
NTC's Dictionary of Canadian French
Au courant: Expressions for Communicating in
  Everyday French

**German**
Schöffler-Weis German and English Dictionary
Klett German and English Dictionary
Getting Started in German
German Verbs and Essentials of Grammar
Guide to German Idioms
Street-wise German
Nice 'n Easy German Grammar
German à la Cartoon
NTC's Dictionary of German False Cognates

**Italian**
Zanichelli Super-Mini Italian and English
  Dictionary
Zanichelli New College Italian and English
  Dictionary
Getting Started in Italian
Italian Verbs and Essentials of Grammar

**Greek**
NTC's New College Greek and English
  Dictionary

**Latin**
Essentials of Latin Grammar

**Hebrew**
Everyday Hebrew

**Chinese**
Easy Chinese Phrasebook and Dictionary

**Korean**
Korean in Plain English

**Polish**
The Wiedza Powszechna Compact Polish and
  English Dictionary

**Swedish**
Swedish Verbs and Essentials of Grammar

**Russian**
Complete Handbook of Russian Verbs
Essentials of Russian Grammar
Business Russian
Basic Structure Practice in Russian

**Japanese**
Easy Kana Workbook
Easy Hiragana
Easy Katakana
101 Japanese Idioms
Japanese in Plain English
Everyday Japanese
Japanese for Children
Japanese Cultural Encounters
Nissan's Business Japanese

**"Just Enough" Phrase Books**
Chinese, Dutch, French, German, Greek,
  Hebrew, Hungarian, Italian, Japanese,
  Portuguese, Russian, Scandinavian,
  Serbo-Croat, Spanish
Business French, Business German, Business
  Spanish

**Audio and Video Language Programs**
Just Listen 'n Learn Spanish, French,
  German, Italian, Greek, and Arabic
Just Listen 'n Learn...Spanish,
  French, German PLUS
Conversational...Spanish, French, German,
  Italian, Russian, Greek, Japanese, Thai,
  Portuguese in 7 Days
Practice & Improve Your...Spanish, French,
  Italian, and German
Practice & Improve Your...Spanish, French,
  Italian, and German PLUS
Improve Your...Spanish, French, Italian, and
  German: The P&I Method
VideoPassport French
VideoPassport Spanish
How to Pronounce...Spanish, French,
  German, Italian, Russian, Japanese
  Correctly

## PASSPORT BOOKS
a division of *NTC Publishing Group*
Lincolnwood, Illinois USA